AF223924

Responsible Business

The Pathway to a
Great Workplace Culture

Nick A. Shepherd

Jim Bignal

Copyright © 2023 Eduvision Inc., Jannas Publications, Responsible Business 2030, Great Workplace Cultures, J. Bignal and N. Shepherd
All rights reserved.

No part of this book may be reproduced, or stored in a retrieval system, or transmitted in any form or by any means, electronic, mechanical, photocopying, recording, or otherwise, without express written permission of the publisher.

ISBN 978-1-7781309-6-0

Cover design by:
EduVision Inc. / Jim Bignal

Responsible Business 2030 (RBP 2030) is a UK based Community Interest Company. This book draws heavily on their responsible business concepts outlined at
https://www.responsiblebusiness2030.com/

Jannas Publications / Eduvision Inc. worked in conjunction with RBP 2030 to create this book, which is based on UK approaches but with application to business globally.

DARE

TO

CARE

Run a
Responsible Business

Dedication

To all the people I have met in my life. Thank you for crossing my path and in some way or another, adding to my rich tapestry of life experiences.

To my friend and mentor Dr. Peter Smyth who has spent many years leading me through the journey of learning about the complexity of people. As Peter says, "you have to love people."

To Jim Bignal, Founder of "Responsible Business 2030" thank you for helping me find a home for my passion around organizational culture in the Responsible Business movement. Much of this book is Jim's original thinking combined with my passion for business management, models, and culture. Let us hope we can change the world!

To my family – especially my wife Janet, children Sarah, Lee-Jane and David, and to my grandchildren Ben, Lindsay and Erin. We are all on the journey that we call life. Live. Love, and may we all succeed in our passion for building a better world.

Table of Contents

Foreword

Business holds an important place in society. While its' creation centres around economic value and wealth creation, it benefits us by providing products and services that society wants or needs. Being "market driven" it has a core role in idea creation and through this encourages innovation and creativity.

A core driver for business is wealth creation which is instrumental in attracting investment. While this focus on the investor remains important, the impact of business activities on the wider well-being of society is also important. In recent years this balance between investor and society has come under criticism.

There are many descriptors for the necessary improvements we believe will benefit both business and society. Stakeholder capitalism; inclusive capitalism; conscious capitalism; purposeful capitalism and others. We like responsible capitalism but prefer responsible business.

Business needs to "clean up its' act" and restore a more effective balance between investors and other "stakeholders" – those who have an impact on or are impacted by its activities. This book will establish the need for change and take the reader through ideas, activities, and actions necessary to restore a balance between investor needs and those of society – to become more responsible. This book is also about corporate culture; what it is, how to understand it and how to create and sustain it. It is not a program. It is not a one-time project or a tool. IT is a way of thinking that embodies caring and respect for those and the world around us.

This book embraces the importance of business purpose – but believes that this MUST combine both a social and a commercial purpose.

There are two elements to this book. The early chapters, the 5-step process lays out what we believe are the foundations needed to "fix the problem." Later in the book we have added chapters for those who want to dig deeper. These explain the business case for change, and how our principles MUST be embedded within the basic business model. Without this integration, our ideas may just become another project and never really become "the way we do things around here." In other words, a responsible business culture.

Be the change.

Nick Shepherd
Ottawa, Canada, 2023

Jim Bignal
Wargrave, Berkshire, England, 2023

1 Introduction

Responsible Business and the Great Workplace Culture Initiative

<u>Dare to Care</u>

Broadening Business Purpose

This book is about the business sector and its responsibility as a global citizen to help solve some of the many problems confronting our society and the planet. We provide some solutions.

There are some who believe that business sector's sole aim is to make a profit and as long as they stay within the law that is fine. We are not suggesting these businesses have a total disregard for people and business issues (after all they are aware of the potential negative impact of social media), and only focus on profit. But we are concerned that too many investors and business leaders do not feel that people and planet issues are their responsibility. They argue this should be left to government regulation.

Others disagree including the authors of this book. We think our position is superbly described through the quote from Elizabeth Warren, an American politician and former law professor who is currently the senior United States senator from Massachusetts, serving since 2013

> "There is nobody in this country who got rich on their own. Nobody. You built a factory out there - good for you. But I want to be clear. You moved your goods to market on roads the rest of us paid for. You hired workers the rest of us paid to educate. You were safe in your factory because of police forces and fire forces that the rest of us paid for. You didn't have to worry that marauding bands would come and seize everything at your factory... Now look. You built a factory and it turned into something terrific or a great idea - God bless! Keep a hunk of it. But part of the underlying social contract is you take a hunk of that and pay forward for the next kid who comes along."

Of course, it is about much more than paying fair taxes - although that would be a great start! It is about the business sector accepting its responsibility for the negative impact of its' business on people and the planet – commonly called externalities. Essentially, it is about treating all people fairly and respectfully and respecting the climate.

Before the profit focused leaders throw up their hands in despair, we acknowledge it is also about making an ethical profit.

In this book, we argue that **people, planet, and profit are <u>a responsibility and not a choice</u>**. We make the case for change and provide a solution on how this triple purpose can be achieved.

Capitalism is at a crossroads.

More and more of the general public are becoming disenchanted. They are looking for companies to be more focussed on their responsibilities to their people, to wider society and to the planet, as well as making an ethical profit. So, capitalism is at a crossroads, with the growing perception, particularly with the younger generations, that business is failing in its obligations especially to society and the planet.

They believe that capitalism as currently practised, is badly in need of reform! We agree – even though we are seasoned businesspeople with long careers behind us!

Why this disenchantment?

Every day seems to bring a new corporate scandal - companies not paying their fair rate of tax or not paying their suppliers on time; excessive pay for senior executives (a FTSE100 Chief Executive is paid 165 times more than a nurse who saves our lives and cares for our sick); deceptive fuel emission "compliance;" miss-selling products and services; poor pay, abuse of workers and so on. Chapter 9 that gives more in-depth background on problems like unethical behaviour.

In the workplace, poor mental and physical health are also an increasing problem with huge cost implications to individuals, society, and the state.

While the concept of climate change is now generally accepted, even within the business sector, evidence from COP 27, suggests that business is still not doing enough to prevent catastrophic consequences.

There are structural challenges facing our society too. Multi-national companies are becoming worryingly influential and powerful.

New business models including the "gig" economy, with their zero-hours contracts, are on the increase.

People worry about robots, and the Internet of Things and Artificial Intelligence - (collectively called the Fourth Industrial Revolution). Many people fear for the continued existence of their jobs. Also, social media, although great in many ways, is creating new challenges.

These changes are not inherently bad – disruption in the past has often been to the long-term benefit of society. But companies have a responsibility to avoid, wherever possible, adverse consequences to people and planet in the pursuit of profit throughout this process of disruption. Change needs to be managed with the impact on ALL stakeholders considered.

Just to be clear what is a stakeholder?

> *A stakeholder is anyone who has an interest in, or is impacted by decisions, actions, and activities of another – whether an individual or a business entity.*

Against this backdrop, in the UK, the national health system and social services are stretched to the limit. There is an inadequate housing stock. There are big challenges in the educational system. Financial support for the disadvantaged is being reduced, plus the threat of climate change - and so on. This is not just a UK issue. The challenges are worldwide.

Many people are surviving on low incomes and are only "just about managing". Some are not managing, even when they have a job, and are relying on foodbanks and other charities, to survive. Even members of the armed forces in countries like Canada and the US are having to use food banks.

Anger over the levels of inequality is increasing. The numbers of working poor and children in poverty are increasing with mental health problems unacceptably high. People complain that "The middle class is shrinking, the rich are getting richer and the poor getting poorer."

This situation is clearly intolerable and unacceptable in the 21st Century. The solutions to these problems are not just down to the business sector – all sectors have a role to play especially government and civil society. However, the business sector plays such an enormous role in our society – as the United Nations stated when it issued the globally endorsed Social Development Goals:

> *No matter how large or small, and regardless of their industry, all companies can contribute to the SDGs. While the scale and scope of the global goals is unprecedented, the fundamental ways that business can contribute remain unchanged. The UN Global Compact asks companies to first do business responsibly and then pursue opportunities to solve societal challenges through business innovation and collaboration.*

We agree. Business MUST be part of the solution. Not by changing the idea of capitalism but by changing the way it has drifted away from serving society.

There is some reason for hope.

There is a growing movement of people advocating reform of the business sector. People and organisations who believe things need to change. They have concerns about free-market capitalism and its apparent lack of ethical values. Its' pursuit of short-term profit, low investment in R&D and innovation and poor productivity. ***They do, however, have a vision that capitalism, a 21st Century version of capitalism, can be a force for good***.

More and more people want to work for organisations whose values represent their own. They feel passionately that businesses should focus on people, planet, and profit, and are prepared to work hard to achieve these objectives. They are looking for some **purpose** in their work.

This progressive movement is advocating a fundamental *culture change*. It argues that businesses, rather than being focused on a single purpose, to make a profit, needs to become more socially and environmentally responsible. To value and respect the people that work for them. To play a part in the local community and wider society, and to make the world a better place for future generations.

A new approach to business – a great workplace culture

This needs a "refreshed" approach to business. This will entail, at least in many companies, building a culture focused on a happy, motivated, and creative workforce, with great jobs, fair pay, and ethics-based decision-making. Where there is a shared sense of individual and company purpose embedded in the DNA of the organisation.

A place where people are the drivers of value creation, and where moral values predominate in decision-making. Values such as personal responsibility, respect for others, integrity, fairness, and kindness.

Workplaces where inclusivity predominates. Places where everyone feels they can contribute to a greater purpose other than just making a profit. A place where there is a balance between social responsibilities (to society and the environment) and to generating a reasonable, sustainable, and ethical profit.

There are some solid signs that the needed changes are starting to be recognized and that some progress is already being made.

- Shareholders and other investors are increasingly demanding greater transparency and accountability on both climate change and social issues.
- Governments are strengthening laws around areas such as diversity, equity, and inclusion.

- Regulators are increasing accountability and are demanding more than financial performance reporting.
- Both regulators and governments are stepping in and taking action where non-compliance is occurring.
- The UN has gained international agreement to adopt a plan (the United Nations Sustainable Development Goals) for achieving a better future for all — laying out a path over the next 15 years to end extreme poverty, fight inequality and injustice, and protect our planet.

This is progress but is it happening fast enough?

We all accept the world is changing fast and many fear some of these changes are for the worse – climate change, inequality, poverty, lack of education, forced migration– but is business responding in an adequate way relative to its potential?

Some might suggest either "no" or as a minimum progress is too slow. Some executives are taking action, but some seem to believe there are no problems and that their current solutions are adequate.

Ask yourself the question – are these situations acceptable when we are already 20% into the 21st century?

How about caring about our people?
- Almost 60% of people living in households (in the UK) where at least one person works, are in poverty (Health Foundation, 2022)
- Although we all "clapped for the care workers" after COVID, almost 25% of all jobs in adult social care sector are zero-hour contracts. (Zero Hours Justice, 2021).
- Only 51% of organisations take a strategic approach to employee well-being (CIPD Health and Well-being at work report, 2022).
- 98% of FTSE 350 companies have no worker representation at board level (FRC Work Engagement Report, 2021).

- 86% of workers in the private sector are not protected by a collective agreement (BEIS Trade Union Membership Report, 2021).
- Almost half FTSE top 100 companies have NO female senior executives. (Tortoise Responsibility100 Index, 2022).

How about caring about the planet?

- Current emissions reductions efforts are only half of what is needed to meet the Paris agreement aimed at 1.5% warming.
- Only 16 of the FTSE 100 have set targets that align to the 1.5% goal (Tortoise Responsibility100 Index, 2022).
- 50% of the public in the US believe that the government (Biden) is not doing enough for climate change (AP-NORC Poll, 2022)
- Only 23% of survey respondents say businesses are doing enough to address the world's climate challenges (Salesforce survey, UK, and USA, 2021)
- 52 per cent of UK businesses don't currently have a clear CSR (Corporate Social Responsibility) strategy set out. (Fintech Times, 2022).

How about profits?

- In February 2023, Shell reported its highest profits in 115 years. Profits hit $39.9bn (£32.2bn) in 2022, double the previous year's total.
- A cross-party Committee of UK MPs investigating the four major banks, outlined that, despite interest rates rising from 0.25 per cent in January 2022 to four per cent today, all banks offered less than one per cent interest for their "easy access savings accounts."
- Total monetary penalties in the last ten years, for businesses who broke the law, amount to £12.6 billion (Violation Tracker UK, 2022)
- The Violation Tracker's USA's current list of the top ten most penalized companies show fines and penalties that cost $301 BILLION.

- The International Monetary Fund estimates that avoidance of corporation tax is costing national governments between $500 and $600 billion annually.
- Prior to the Boeing 737 Max being grounded in 2019, Boeing shares returned 25% annually (2011-2018) and cash flow rose 33% per year. (Forbes, 2019)
- 400,000 small businesses in the UK face winding up because of late payments by customers. (FSB Small Business Index, 2022).

Overall, it certainly appears that there remain many improvements to be made in the "way the system works" for most people.

The importance of profit

A healthy business sector, one that looks after its people and respects society and the environment and one that makes an ethical profit creates a massive benefit to all humankind.

Businesses making an ethical profit, rather than loss-making, will, in all probability, employ more people, pay better, provide better career progression and are more likely to be sustainable, providing a long-term future for the employees. Profitable businesses are more likely to have a great social purpose and do better, for people and the planet, than businesses that are struggling.

Profit, yes but not at a cost to people and planet

However, we do not believe that it is right to push for profit at the expense of people or the planet. Clearly, the most urgent action required NOW relates to the reduction of CO2 emissions.

But action is also required on many other social and behavioural issues. We argue that resolving these big challenges of our time is a responsibility and not a choice.

While we accept the importance of profit, a focus on mainly profit-oriented strategy can often, and in fact does, have a negative effect on people and planet issues such as low and unfair pay, mental health issues, toxic workplace atmosphere and an irresponsible attitude to climate change.

Good corporate citizens

So, we are looking for businesses to become good corporate citizens: responsible businesses with a holistic strategy accepting their triple responsibility towards people, planet, and profit issues. It is the purpose of this book is to help companies achieve this triple purpose objective and to make **responsible business commonplace by 2030**.

This objective, to aspire to be a responsible business, must become the primary purpose of an organisation. It is self-evident that more working people making responsible decisions day-in, day-out will make the world a better place to live and work. No-one can do everything but, for sure, everyone can do something.

We know there are increasingly large numbers of passionate and visionary people who support this objective (to be a responsible business). These progressive and passionate people (we call them Champions for Change) are prepared to play their part and take action to strongly advocate responsible business within their organisation and to challenge any irresponsible behaviour and decision-making when they see it.

We argue that it is only with the foundation of a great workplace culture, that businesses will be able to make the changes the world so desperately and urgently needs. The purpose of this book is to offer a workable, practical solution to creating a great workplace culture.

The case for responsible business

It seems only right that businesses need to take responsibility for the consequences of all decisions that they make. The case for responsible business is inarguable for most caring people but, fortunately, there is also a very strong business case too (see Chapter 9).

There is already a growing understanding in the business world of the importance of balancing people and planet with profitability.

So, a move from a primarily profit focussed business model to one focused on all stakeholders must be achieved without adversely affecting both people and the planet i.e., it needs to be a just transition.

There is evidence that companies with this broader focus make bigger profits and are valued more highly than competitors. See Alex Edmans Book "Grow the Pie[1] Balancing people, planet and profit – a just transition".

Fortunately, if Alex Edmans and many others are correct, the rewards of this triple purpose focus, will likely be, a happier, more productive workforce with a long-term future with the company, a fairer society, a better planet, and good sustainable profit.

So, what are the solutions?

It's all about culture.

There are literally thousands of great organisations (for-profit and not-for profit) working in the purpose driven sector yet few place a strategic focus on the importance of workplace culture.

---

[1] https://www.growthepie.net/

We argue that it is only from the foundations of a great workplace culture that the business sector can make decisions and take actions that can reverse some of the national and global challenges.

It is from a culture focused on corporate purpose, social as well as environmental, underpinned by a happy, engaged, responsible and creative workforce that amazing things can happen.

A great workplace culture will not come about by accident. It will require a dedicated commitment to create a working environment where everyone treats each other with respect and compassion and feels empowered, engaged, and valued.

It is important to note that any culture change initiative must be part of a holistic and sustained strategy. Unless it is tackled holistically, it is likely to fail. It seems that over 70% of culture change initiatives fail. It is essential that the initiative is supported by management, be employee centric and utilize the inspirational and creative energy of your "Champions for Change". However, whatever the route, most responsible businesses, in the long-term, will survive, many irresponsible businesses will not.

We believe, that from a great workplace culture amazing things can happen. Our approach. laid out in this book is, we believe, simple.

The Pillars **People, Planet Profit**

The Foundations **Responsible decision making by all, founded on Clarity of Purpose and Code of Ethics, and turned into reality through: ACTION**

This is our "framework for change" that the following chapters explain.

Some thought-provoking questions.

In this introduction we have made several statements. Think about these. Discuss them with others. Your responses may start your journey. "Let's chat" means that you should talk this over with others to obtain their opinion before you answer!

The suggestion	Agree	Dis-agree	Let's Chat
People, planet, and profit are a responsibility and not a choice			
Climate action is becoming critical and the time for talk is past. Action is needed NOW.			
Capitalism is at a crossroads			
More and more of the general public and employees are becoming disenchanted (with business)			
However, it seems not enough business leaders see the need for change.			
In the workplace, poor mental and physical health are an increasing problem.			
Change needs to be managed with the impact on ALL stakeholders considered.			
Anger over the levels of inequality is increasing			

The suggestion	Agree	Dis-agree	Let's Chat
A new approach to business is needed, where greater emphasis is placed on responsible decision-making with regards to people and planet issues.			
Is business responding in an adequate way relative to its potential?			
Profitable businesses are more likely to have a great social purpose and do better than businesses struggling to survive			
Most of us know that the time for action is now.			
It seems only right that businesses need to take responsibility for adverse consequences of the decisions they make			
We believe, that from a great workplace culture amazing this can happen.			
Unless passionate activists demand action from their employers today, then these big challenges will never be resolved.			
We believe that businesses need to be run for the long-term and that short term profit maximization is often not in the interests of people or the planet and / or investors			

The suggestion	Agree	Dis-agree	Let's Chat
We believe that although there is some progress towards a more responsible form of capitalism, but that…(next question)			
Action is not being taken on sufficient scale and certainly not quickly enough.			

After working through the discussion questions, you may want to give yourself a score. There are eighteen questions. If your score fourteen or more as agree you are well on your way to being a Champion for Change!

2 A framework for real change

2.1   It's all about the culture.

There are literally thousands of great organisations (for-profit and not-for-profit) in the business sector, claiming to be purpose driven, but very few focus on the importance of workplace culture.

Culture together with corporate purpose and employee engagement are becoming popular themes, which might lead one to suspect that the required changes are underway. Maybe. But too often purpose remains focused on investors and commercial issues. Employee engagement in spite of all the talk remains stuck at embarrassingly low levels (about 30% in the US). The culture in many organisations is not yet the positive foundation for success the way it needs to be.

We argue that it is only from the _foundations of a great workplace culture_ focused on people, planet, and ethical profit that the business sector can make decisions and take actions that can reverse some of the national and global challenges.

It is from a culture focused on "total" corporate purpose - commercial, social, and environmental, underpinned by a happy, engaged, responsible and creative workforce, that amazing things can happen.

A great workplace culture will not come about by accident. It will require a dedicated commitment to create a working environment where everyone treats each other with respect and compassion and feel empowered, engaged, and valued. We can all make a difference. We can be the change that is needed.

This Photo by Unknown Author is licensed under CC BY

It's time for change!

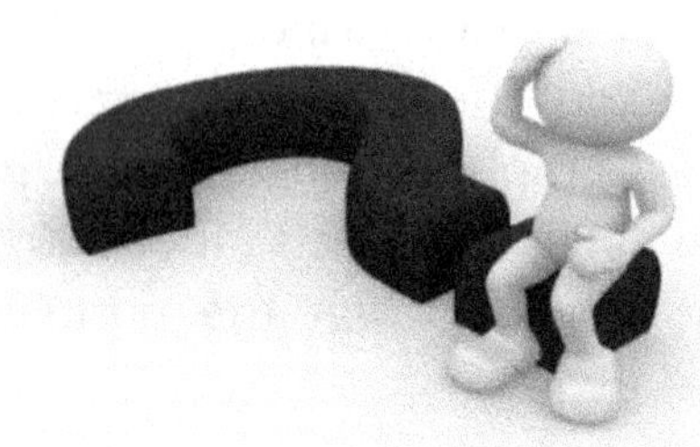

Don't just sit and think about it. By now we hope you can see that change is needed. It only happens when someone takes action.

Imagine a WORKPLACE CULTURE where:

- The principles of basic human rights are foremost in personal actions and decision-making at all levels of the organisation.
- Its people treat each other with respect and compassion.
- There is a diverse and inclusive workplace where people feel valued, empowered, engaged.
- Everyone is encouraged and supported to be creative, and collaborate, and are enabled to thrive and lead a balanced life.

- There is an emphasis on the physical, mental, and moral wellbeing of its people through providing a psychological and physically safe workplace environment.
- There are fair and transparent processes of governance with a focus on providing purposeful work, training, equality of opportunity and opportunities for personal growth.
- **Social purpose** is indelibly printed into the DNA of the organisation; essentially to serve society and to respect the environment.
- Everyone understands and accepts their responsibilities towards themselves, their organization and its commercial objectives, society, and the environment.

> "We are past (asking) should we!. The question (now) is how?"
>
> — **Dr. Mehmood Khan, Distinguished Business Leader** (quote from when he was Vice-Chairman of PepsiCo).

These changes will come about. Concern is building over inequality and perceived unfairness. Time frames for climate action are shrinking.

> **We all write each others' story**

If we believe there is an issue, each of us needs to act. To figure out how we, individually can be the catalyst for change.

> **"If Not Me, Then Who"**
> *Mantra of the Travis Manion Foundation (TMF)*

Are you a Champion for Change?

This book is part of a framework of approaches, looking to create great workplace cultures using the passion and enthusiasm of people who want to, and feel they can, contribute to making the world a better place.

We call these people **"Champions for Change".**

Do you want a great workplace culture that has a happy, well-paid, highly motivated, and well-trained workforce, supported by a strong ethical culture prioritising compassion, respect, responsibility, and fairness?

Do you want to work in or lead a company that has a strong social purpose that:
- creates a positive social impact.
- helps resolve the world's climate challenges.

Do you believe that you can (working closely with your colleagues) contribute to building such a company?

Then you are A CHAMPION FOR CHANGE

The Great Workplace Culture initiative

A core and essential part of our proposed approach to change is <u>The Great Workplace Culture Initiative</u>. This is focused on creating such a workplace environment where people enjoy their job and feel that their work has a purpose outside of purely commercial objectives.

Our approach proposes a five-stage pathway enabling "Champions for Change" to create a workplace where people love their job, are happy, fulfilled, fairly treated, and feel that their work has a social value and helps make the world a better place.

We know that over 70% of culture change programmes fail. We are confident that utilising the following core principles for successful culture change, lasting results can be achieved.

- **Responsible decision-making**
- **Ethics**
- **Action**
- **Purpose (Social)**

It is critical to remember that involving employees in this process, will improve the chances of success.

This programme will provide our "Champions for Change" with a step-by-step and holistic approach to creating a great workplace culture.

We are not suggesting that Champions can just think up an idea and expect people to rally round. Support from others will be needed as will support from both management and where applicable, owners and / or Board of Directors.

This book will show you how champions may emerge at any level in the business, but that certain steps are needed to gain "traction" for the desired changes.

> Companies can use this suggested pathway or develop their own – the important thing is that any culture change initiative must be part of a holistic and sustained strategy. It must be supported by management, be employee-centric and utilise the inspirational and creative energy of your "Champions for Change".

The essential conditions for a culture change

It is a well-known fact that in ANY change initiative there are some critical and essential foundations for success. In developing an approach to changing the underlying culture to reflect clearly understood values that underpin decision making at all levels, the following will be important.

Leadership buy-in to a sustained and holistic culture change strategy.
Where the Board publicly commits to a sustained and holistic strategy focused on creating a great workplace culture by empowering the "Champions for Change" and giving them the psychological and financial support to create this change.

Individual and personal responsibility
An understanding and acceptance that we, at all levels of seniority, must take personal responsibility for the decisions and actions we take as individuals with these decisions based on the Company's Values and Code of Ethics

Culture Change Committee

Where the "Champions for Change" form a dedicated committee ("Culture Committee"?) with a clear mandate from senior management to create a great workplace culture. A committee member needs to report directly to the Board.

Culture change involving everybody.

Where the development of a structured culture change strategy is co-created via open discourse engaging everybody (who is interested) not just senior managers.

Code of Ethics

Where the Company's Values and Code of Ethics are co-created (or an existing code updated) with anyone interested, based on views garnered from via surveys, focus groups and Town Hall meetings.

Company's social purpose

Where the Company's Social Purpose is co-created: identifying how the company contributes to making the world a better place to live and work. In other words, why the company exists outside of "just" making a profit. By covering its responsibility to society, its people, customers, all other stakeholders, the local community and to the environment.

2.2   Our approach is simple.

Let's keep this simple. We are not upending business but ensuring its purpose is clear and its foundations are solid.

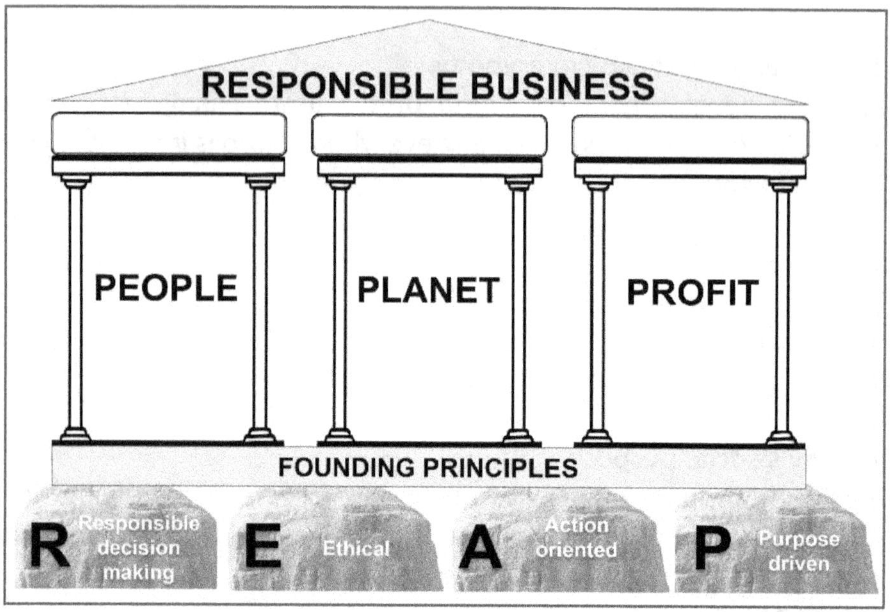

A Responsible Business focused on people, planet, and profit, through responsible decision making that is ethical, action oriented and purpose driven.

That's it.

Not to say that it won't be hard. The toughest part will be ensuring that intentions are converted into action. Leadership will play one of the most important roles.

Some thought-provoking questions.
What are your thoughts and reflections on this chapter? Take some time to consider and possibly discuss with others.

The suggestion	Agree	Dis-agree	Let's Chat
Do you think business is "Purpose driven?"			
Does the purpose of business include social responsibility?			
Over 70% of culture change initiatives fail. True or False? Why? (Discuss)			
Are you or can you be a "Champion for Change?"			
Would you say people that you work with make responsible decisions?			
Are decisions guided by ethical considerations as well as being commercially viable?			
Could you start a "Culture Change Committee" in your organization?			

Let's Go!

3 The Five Step process to create a Great Workplace Culture

An organization's culture is often referred to "as the way we do things around here." If, through pressure for change, it is decided that "the way things are happening around here could be much better," as outlined in the previous chapter, then a culture change is what's needed.

Culture change is at the heart of a responsible business.

For a culture change initiative to be successful, and change the course of an organization it:

- Must be supported by management.
- Must be part of a holistic and sustained strategy.,
- Must be employee centric.
- Must utilise the inspirational and creative energy of your culture change champions.
- Requires a vision of what the future might look like coupled with the willingness, ability, and resources to take action.

The 5-step process outlined in this chapter provides a simple framework for the essential activities to develop the vision with an emphasis on action.

The five steps are in fact a continuous loop with the fifth step being continual improvement, because an effective culture will include learning and ideas of better ways to do things. It is a continual process of iteration.

The first four steps are based on a simple acronym using the word REAP for

- **R**esponsibility,
- **E**thics,
- **A**ction, and
- **P**urpose.

Continual improvement – the fifth step, reconnects to the beginning, to build a reflective process that is ALWAYS looking for better ways to operate.

3.1   Champions for change

In the previous chapter we introduced the idea of champions for change. These "champions" can come from anywhere within the organisation.

While management or the board is expected to recognize a need for change and "start the ball rolling," a responsible business will be listening closely to all sources that indicate that things should be improved.

That's why part of being a responsible business is being open, aware, and responsive to key stakeholders, such as employees, suppliers, customers, and the local community.

Don't limit the potential for ideas to traditional sources. While employees are critical stakeholders, organisations need to think about their whole workforce – including both full time employees but also part-time, casual, contract, seasonal and all others who provide human input.

Both suppliers and customers can also be rich sources of ideas. Closer relationships based on concepts of partnering have provided individuals working for both suppliers and customers with the potential for great ideas about how work processes and relationships can be improved. This is where REAL change in culture occurs.

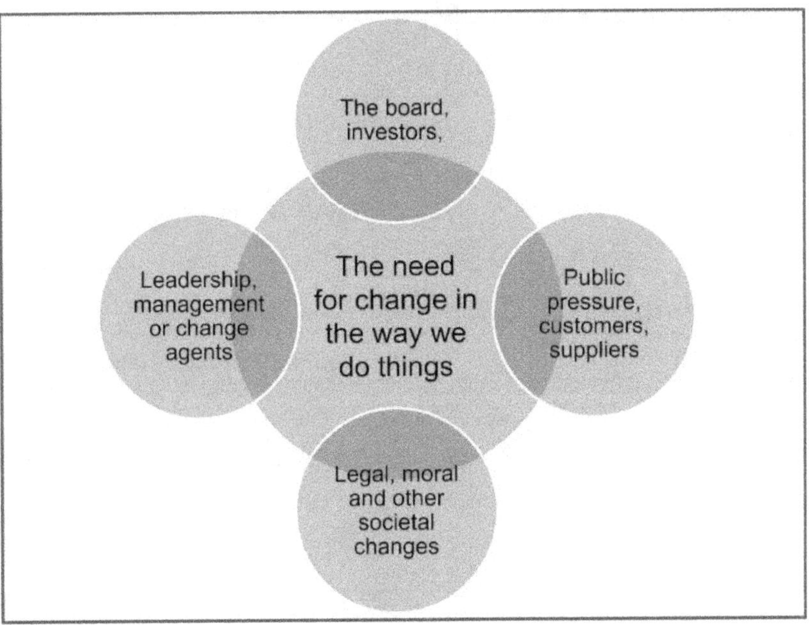

No matter where the call for change is coming from, developing the zeal, ideas and enthusiasm for change must be channelled into some type of framework to convert intent into action. This starts with getting "management on board" to take action and respond. This takes us to the need for an approach such as the five-step model that we suggest.

Although companies may well develop their own pathway, the important thing to remember is that successful culture change must be part of a holistic and sustained strategy, actively supported by management and utilising the inspirational and creative energy of Champions for Change.

Chapter 11 provides additional materials and explanations about this concept of holistic change and how it must become solidly embedded within your organizations existing business model. A Responsible Business is not an idea you "bolt on" to the ways things are currently done. It is the foundation of how EVERYTHING will be done in the future.

3.2   Summary of the five-step process.

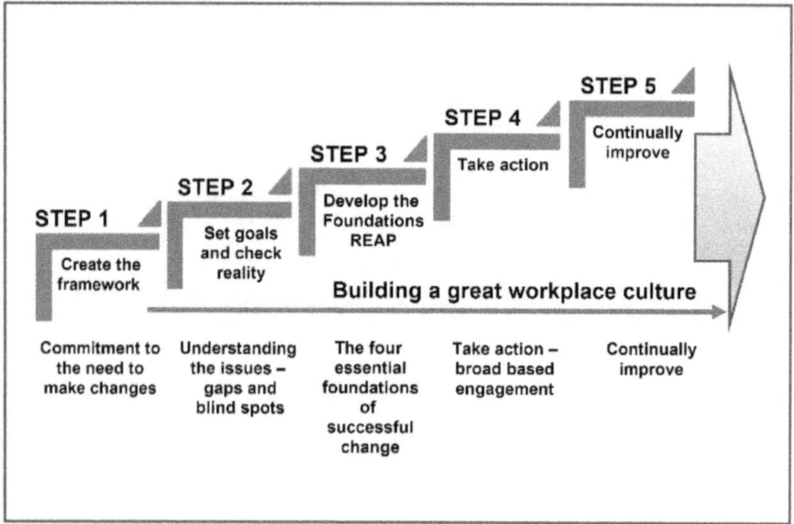

Step 1 – Creating a Framework

The five step approach rests upon a commitment to change from the board, management, and the champion(s) for change.

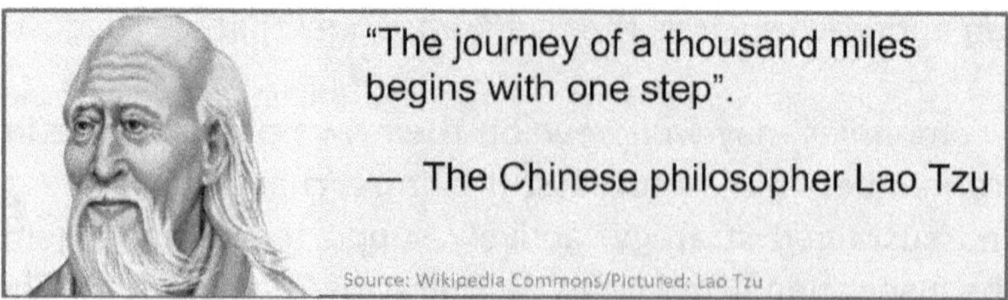

Boards and senior management buy-in to cultural change.

This Stage emphasises the vital importance of Board commitment and senior management buy-in, to this Great Workplace Culture initiative. It must be part of a sustained and holistic strategy using the passion and vision of the company's Champions for Change.

Culture Change Committee

We recommend forming a Culture Change Committee (it need not be called this name). Having a culture change committee, dedicated to a cultural change, and run by passionate individuals, goes a long way to ensuring that the culture change actually happens.

We suggest a structure and define the purpose of this committee. It is imperative that the Culture Change Committee is given the time and financial support they need. This again provides evidence to the employees and others that the Board is serious about the culture change initiative.

Step 2 – Set Goals and Reality Check.

Here we summarise the Culture Change Committee actions, the first major action being to understand employee views about **"where we are now"** (with regards to the culture of the company) and **"where we would like to be"** via an employee survey, pulse surveys, focus groups and other dialogue.

This is the culture gap.

Next an action plan (detailing the purpose, specific issues, the time frame, and costs) is developed and agreed by the Culture Change Committee based on the assessment of the gap. This action plan needs to be approved by the board.

Step 3 – Developing the foundations for culture change. REAP

Step three is about establishing / putting in place the foundation stones of a great workplace culture. These four foundations stones are based on the acronym REAP so that they can be easily remembered.

- **R**esponsibility, an environment where responsible decision-making predominates.
- **E**thics, agreeing the core values and a company code of ethics.
- **A**ction, the importance of taking action (doing something), and
- **P**urpose. Developing the Company's social purpose – why the company exists, in what way does it benefit society.

REAP is all about how leadership turns the idea of being a Responsible Business into operational reality. Both by stating what the organisation stands for and believes in, and by setting policies and procedures, making decisions, and taking action that are seen as authentic, honest, fair and reflect integrity. In short "we do what we say we do."

Step 4 – Take Action

Once the foundations are in place action is needed. In this step we emphasise some key factors for successful culture change focusing on the vital importance of leadership buy-in, an employee centric approach and fair and transparent governance of the company. The importance of continual and transparent communication and effective training is also emphasised.

Step 5 – Continually Improve

Step five emphasises the need for continual improvement of the company's governance. The importance of continual and transparent communication and effective training is also emphasised.

As the culture begins to shift and the "voice of the employee" starts to be heard, opportunities for improvement will start to flow. This will then feed back into re-looking at how the organisation operates and continually making changes. This cultural environment is designed to stimulate ideas, innovation, and creativity. Action will be needed to develop these ideas.

3.3 Important considerations

Commitment to change is a strategic imperative.
A genuine and long-term commitment to change to become a more responsible business is a strategic imperative.

It is not a project with a beginning and an end. It is a shift in the way that business decisions are made. Planning will change – as will execution, measurement and decision making.

A shift towards ALL stakeholders
There has been a much-publicised commitment by business to focus on purpose – yet business has always focused on purpose. Central to this cultural shift is the commitment to more effectively balance shareholder needs and those of other stakeholders.

A responsible business will continue to focus on purpose, yet it will more clearly define this commitment to include both its business purpose and its social purpose.

RESPONSIBLE BUSINESS <u>PURPOSE</u>

**Focus on our core business purpose
(what we do)
PLUS
An equal focus on our social purpose – to behave
and act as a responsible member of society
(how we do it)**

To achieve this "duality of purpose" both definitions must be embedded into every aspect of business governance, leadership, and management. Thus, a new way of thinking must be embedded into the basic business model to sustain the commitment. (See how this works in Chapter 11).

Champions and "Learning to Listen."

Employees have a good idea about what is going on in their business. What reality looks like. As they talk to suppliers, customers, and other departments and locations they learn where problems, issues and challenges exist.

These people are often frustrated when they see examples of changes that need to be made yet their voices are not heard. Sometimes they are embarrassed by how their business acts in their community. Sometimes these people complain but, in many organizations, even if they are listened to, they are not heard. Nobody changes anything. THIS is a central cause of disengaged employees. There is nothing worse than knowing something is going wrong, yet management appears not to do anything about it.

A willingness to be open to workers opinions and ideas is an essential first step. Information and awareness are the food of your champions.

HARNESS THE POWER OF THE PEOPLE

Surely – we already listen to our people, you say.
There are often several barriers to people's voices being heard Central to becoming a responsible business is the realization and acceptance that things can improve. Many CEO's when asked the question will strongly defend their business as already being responsible.

Maybe that's because the CEO is too far removed from what is happening on the front lines. Maybe efforts to raise problems are being suppressed by individual managers?

Maybe they fear that a complaint or observation about something that needs to be changed will be a blemish on their own record. A negative factor to be taken into account in their next performance review. A risk that their bonus might be less than planned.

These issues are not about problem people but about parts of a system that makes it hard for the voice of the employee to be heard.

THE MIND IS LIKE A PARACHUTE – IT ONLY WORKS WHEN ITS OPEN

Building a responsible business must be founded on trust and a willingness to hear and address problems. This starts with an openness to hearing the voice of the employee. Way beyond suggestion schemes – and more of an atmosphere that encourages, promotes, and supports people who speak up. Therefore, a responsible business is founded on "a great workplace culture" where people can feel they are "psychologically safe."

3.4   Do you support your people as Champions of Change?

It is a proven fact that employee engagement can have a major impact on organizational performance. Greater productivity, higher growth rates, less employee turnover, more cooperation, and collaboration.

One of the greatest barriers to achieving employee engagement is employee frustration with their voice not being heard. A desire to become a more responsible business can be kicked off by promoting a climate where the voice of the employee really does start to be heard. Yet so often business is afraid that allowing more employee input would just be negative and create expectations that can't be achieved.

Encouraging employees to speak up is an important starting point – especially if it is accompanied by a commitment from the employees to be a positive part of change? In Appendix 13.1 we provide a document that could be used as a pledge, that employees, who want to start building a case for change could sign.

Encouraging and allowing people who are interested in improving the status quo to sign on to being a responsible business champion or activist will be a great step in encouraging ideas and participation. Once these ideas start flowing, then the framework for change can start to be put in place.

As readers will note this pledge also provides assurance that the efforts of the champion include all three pillars – people, planet, and profit. This is not an anti-profit, anti-capitalism, or anti-business idea. It is about how to make things work better for all.

Some thought-provoking questions.

What are your thoughts and reflections on this chapter? Take some time to consider and possibly discuss with others.

The suggestion	Agree	Dis-agree	Let's Chat
Do you agree with the key points for a successful culture change initiative?			
Do you like "Champion of Change", or do you want to use another name such as Activists?			
There are already people I know who can work with me to start this activity.			
Do the five steps in the process outlined in this chapter seem to make sense to you?			
Do you think there is a "culture gap" in your organization?			
Do the four points in the REAP acronym provide a good foundation for change?			
Do you already have a continuous improvement culture in your organization?			
Do you think your organization is listening to "the voice of the people?"			
Do people who want to change things in your organization REALLY get listened to?			

The suggestion	Agree	Dis-agree	Let's Chat
Is "speaking out" encouraged where you work or is there improvement needed?			

4 Step one: creating the framework.

Step one in the five-step process is an essential starting point to obtain both **management commitment** as well as approval of the board. This step also includes the **creation of a Culture Change Committee** which is formed to carry out the work for step two and into step three.

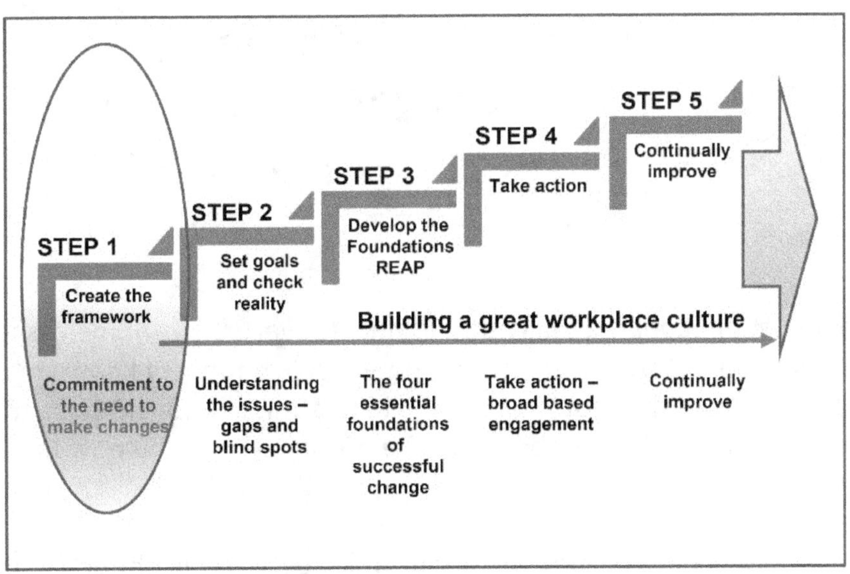

4.1   Commitment from the board and senior management

Think about Step One as "the four "C's". The commitment to these four essential items will start to set a workplace climate within which real change can take place.

- **Commitment** from senior management and the Board
- **Communication** of this commitment
- **Creation** of a psychological safe space
- **Culture** change committee

Think and reflect on these commitments. As a senior manager how are you using your power and influence to affect positive change? How would you be able to respond if your grandchild asks you about what you did?

The question could equally be about "poverty" or homelessness" or discrimination. Would your answer be – "Well, hmm, er I know we talked a lot about it" or "well not much really I am afraid," or even more truthfully "I am so sorry that I contributed to the problems that you now have to live with."

Or will you tell a white lie about the feeble contribution that your generation made to respond to changing the way things were happening at the time? After all, there was CLEAR warnings about what was going to happen. (Possibly all the time thinking in the back of your mind that saying anything might risk the nice bonus that you received which allowed you to pay for your own retirement).

Even better – will your answer be "here are all the things that we did. Where we showed leadership that others adopted and followed?"

Remember - it is evident that any significant and effective culture change within the business sector will only take place with the agreement, passionate support and engaged leadership of senior management. If senior management is not part of the solution, it's part of the problem.

You, – if you are on the Board, a member of the "C" suite, or part of senior management, have the power and influence to affect positive change. TAKE ACTION NOW and avoid having to make excuses later to your granddaughter.

> **Action without vision is only passing time.**
> **Vision without action is merely day dreaming.**
> **But vision with action can change the world.**
> *Nelson Mandela*

So, start by making a commitment to four "C's" – and exercise–your leadership to start the initiative for change:

COMMITMENT from senior management to a strategic and holistic approach to culture change. Management to "walk the talk". This must go beyond mere fiduciary duty. C-suite and senior management buy-in is 100% essential for the success of a culture change program.

- Understand the need for change and get agreement with your senior colleagues to make it happen Learn more about the moral and business case for change (see Chapter 9)
- Update the rewards and incentive systems – including at the board level, with a greater focus on responsible decision making (founded

- on social purpose, business focus and ethical behaviour as a minimum).
- Leaders need to actively demonstrate their commitment. There is nothing more damaging to a culture change initiative than leaders who fail to set a good example.
- Real effective strategic and long-lasting change starts with, and requires a commitment to good governance.
- Senior management must be committed to the successful shift to a value led and ethics-based culture at all levels of management.

To ensure success, it is essential that the commitment to become increasingly responsible is led and supported by management, is people-centric, and utilises the inspirational and creative energy of your "Culture Change Champions."

COMMUNICATION of this commitment to the new culture change initiative to the entire workforce and other stakeholders and encourage the "Champions for Change" to step forward.

- Make a public commitment to colleagues and other stakeholders to cultural change or renewal with a focus on people and planet as well as commercial objectives. (See suggested Board "Memo to all staff" in the appendix 13.2, signed by the Board and the CEO).
- Constantly reinforce this written commitment with actions that reinforce the statement. Asking "how are we doing?" "How can we help?" "What more can we do?"

CREATION of a psychologically safe space where people are free to speak up about issues important to them.

- Open up – be honest. Express your own feelings. Show understanding and empathy.
- LISTEN – don't just allow people to speak. Listen and take action.

CULTURE CHANGE COMMITTEE (or similar name) to be formed by Champions with direct reporting to the Board.

- Agree the company Values and Code of Ethics in collaboration with colleagues all levels and across all stakeholders.
- Create an environment where all decisions are based on the company values and code of ethics, so this becomes "the way we do things around here."
- Find, encourage, nurture, and support your Champions for Change – the people who will help make this happen.
- Enable and financially support the Culture Change Committee (or whatever name you use).

This first step is the equivalent to the foundations of a building. Unless the foundations are firm and solid anything built on top of them is at risk of failing.

From Wikimedia Commons
https://commons.wikimedia.org/wiki/File:Building_foundation.jpg

We talked about a "holistic" approach – but what does this mean? The original term was often used in medicine, referring to treatment of the whole person rather than just part of the body – the concept being that everything is connected. It has now been adopted for business.

Early applications of the idea were focused on silo-busting and the idea of people working together more effectively. It is more than that.

> ## HOLISTIC APPROACH TO BUSINESS
> Sees the business unit as a whole integrated, inter-dependent system. While different resources are used as system inputs, effective integration makes the whole system greater than the sum of the parts.

In the same way that holistic medicine addresses physical and mental well-being, so a holistic business considers all aspects of both task and behaviour[2].

4.2   Culture Change Committee

Who are "Champions for Change?"
Having a great workplace culture is the essential bedrock of a sustainable company but it seems that over 70% of culture change initiatives fail. Unless a culture change initiative is tackled holistically and is part of a sustained strategy, it will join the many others as an expensive and time-consuming failure.

The ultimate level of management support must include both the senior managers ("C" suite) together with the board. The approach to getting this commitment will vary depending upon where the champion(s) for change are located. Champions for change can come from anywhere within the organisation – but to be effective they must either have or get access to "power and leverage."

---

[2] For more reading on balancing organizational task (business purpose) and behaviour (values and ethics), see the book "Reflective Leaders and High-Performance Organizations,"

"CHAMPIONS" level in organisation	Whose support will be needed to get started
INVESTORS	Driven by the board plus the champion
CEO / C SUITE	Other "C" suite plus convince board
MANAGERS	Need a "C" suite "sponsor plus other managers
EMPLOYEES / OTHERS	Need to convince one or more of the above

Anyone inside or outside an organization can be a "champion of change" but champions must have influence. Without influence at a senior level the required strategic commitment together with the allocation of resources will be impossible.

- Employees and others who want to drive change, must convince either a next level manager or a member of senior management who will then become the "influence champion."
- Managers wanting to drive change, will also need to convince a member of senior management of the need for change.
- The CEO or other senior managers are already able to influence change and will provide the required management leadership; they will also need to convince the board that the shift must be part of a committed strategy.
- One person on the board can be a champion of change and will need to work with the Board and CEO to ensure the shift becomes embedded in strategy. Investors who want to see things change will exert influence through the board.

Real strategic change requires governance commitment and support. As we will see later, this is the "G" in ESG reporting, (so important yet in many situations "missing in action.")

This first stage emphasises the vital importance of senior management and Board commitment to a great workplace culture as part of a sustained and holistic strategy using the passion and vision of the company's Champions for Change. We recommend forming a Culture Change Committee (it need not be called this name) and suggest a structure and purpose for this committee.

Setting up the Culture Change Committee

To reinforce the people-centric aspects of wanting to change, a Culture Change Committee (or equivalent) must be established, that will report to the board. This is a powerful approach to opening the channels to "the voice of the people" – allowing the workforce to raise honest issues that they believe are inconsistent with acting like a responsible business. There will be several aspects to be agreed:

Agree Membership of the Culture Change Committee
The MOST important membership criteria will be a passion for genuine and sustainable culture change – people who are Champions for change. This might include:

- Champions from all parts of the business.
- A non-executive director or an alternative direct link to the board.
- People from HR.
- People from Internal Audit.
- Be on the lookout for diversity of thought.

Appoint officers and agree their specific responsibilities.
- A title for the project/initiative.
- Agree the terms of reference and statement of purpose of the committee.
- Determine roles required and key responsibilities.
- Create a communication strategy: to employees and other stakeholders including investors.

Establish committee goals and objectives.
- Establish a provisional timeframe for action.
- Create a plan setting measurable and achievable targets. Publish the plan.
- Establish some key priorities – including where possible some immediate item actions to be addressed (low hanging fruit approach)
- Agree a system that ensures agreed actions actually happen and can be sustained by being embedded in the governance and DNA of the company.

Agree operating protocols.
- Agree housekeeping issues.
- Regular (and frequent, at least initially) meeting times. Meetings should, ideally, be during normal worktimes.
- Establish a reporting line to the board.
- Establish the budget.
- Create some quick wins maybe on environmental issues.

It is important that momentum is maintained. Great communications, regular meetings and "quick wins" can set the stage for a growing belief that change is possible. Surveys suggest that regular and frequent meetings play an integral part in ensuring a successful culture change initiative.

4.3 Building engagement with employees

Another key foundation for the framework is to ensure employee involvement and engagement. There are several ideas that might be implemented to demonstrate the strategic commitment to change. These will include:

- Ensuring that the board communication is sent out personally to every individual (see example 13.2 in Appendix).

- Holding a leadership "town hall" to announce the commitment.
- Identifying both a board member plus a member of the executive team that have been designated to move the initiative forward.
- Encouraging broad participation in the culture change team.
- Holding departmental kick-off meetings to discuss ideas that might be raised with the culture change team.
- Establishing an internal social media platform for people to communicate about the initiative.
  - Posting the goals and objectives of the culture change team.
  - Setting up a website and blog for people to post more detailed ideas and suggestions.
  - Publishing the goals, activities, progress, and achievements of the company in addressing core issues.
- Broadening out the Culture Change Committee as more volunteers start to become involved with specific task teams i.e., sub-committees on climate change, DE&I, wellbeing etc.

While individual champions might be able to act as a catalyst to get change started, they need to also find and encourage others who are interested to participate. Practical issues such as obtaining agreement on when meetings can be held need to be addressed.

How to build support

Champions may want to think about how they start to recruit others into the change initiative. One approach used in the consulting industry is to start with those who don't need convincing,

Most organizations have a workforce that follows a typical bell curve – some people are always "drivers for change" pushing ideas while others are quite happy the way things are.

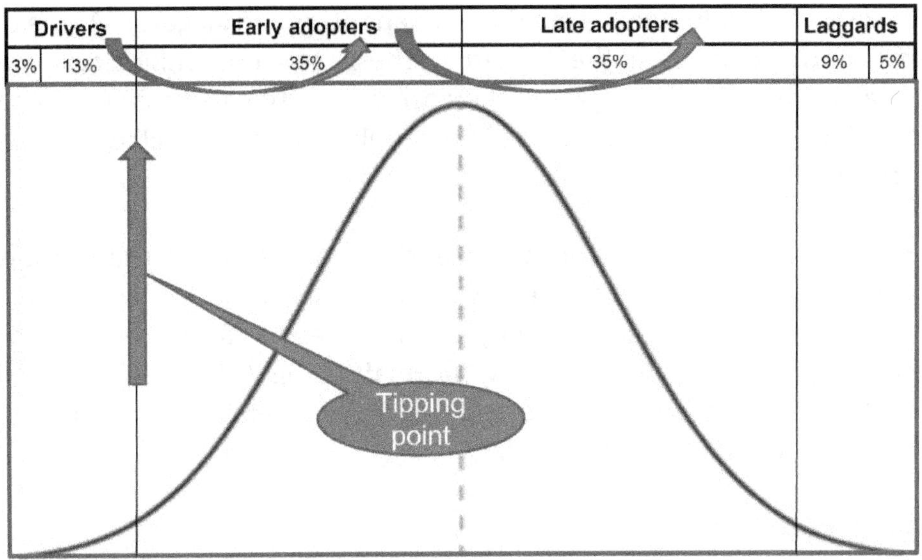

Drivers and early adopters

Initially many employees may be sceptical that real change will happen. *"Oh, just another management initiative"* one might hear. *"Just keep your head down and this will pass."* Others may say *"You go first. I am keeping my head down until I see what happens."*

Our champions will initially come from the enthusiastic "driver's" category – in the chart the 3%. But to get the initiative moving they will need others. Additional champions might also come from the next group – the 13% who want to see change happen but are busy with other things and even may be a bit sceptical. But they won't need convincing of the need for change. This 16% (early adopters) is our core group of change champions.

The next group of "early adopters" are ready for change – but just don't want to "lead" the work. They will start to demonstrate support once the drivers show enthusiasm and support.

Late adopters and laggards
After the early adopters, come the later adopters and laggards. At the other end of the curve are the laggards. These can not only block change initiatives but if not recognized they can take actions that cause a change initiative to fail. Sometimes these people might be called "corporate terrorists."

The reality in many organisations is that both early and late adopters represent the majority of the population that is "sitting on the fence" waiting to see what happens. They key to success is starting on the left and engaging people across the curve from left to right. Early successes from the "drivers and early adopters will build momentum for change. This process leads to the "tipping point."

The tipping point.
Once management demonstrates their total support for change and the culture change team is formed and starts to operate, a "tipping point" will be reached where others in the organization – the fence sitters who tend to be early adopters (they are a bit less risk adverse than the others) will start to say *"maybe it's' real this time. Yes, count me in. What can I do. I have this idea for what we might do or how we might do it."*

The late adopters then start to see the growing momentum and they now start to rally round. The laggards will then either start to reluctantly get involved (after all most of the rest of the workforce seems to be on board) or they will push back. The final 5% will probably push back and will have to be dealt with "down the road."

4.4   The key goals of the Culture Change Committee

The boards letter to employees announcing the formation of the Culture Change Committee creates expectations of action. People expect something to happen. While building participation in the committee will be a continual building process, action should start as soon as there are enough passionate and committed people to start data gathering.

The initial work of the culture change committee is to start asking questions and gathering data to assess both the current "culture" of the organization, and to obtain input on how things might change and the views of the employees on what the future culture might look like.

> **Goal of the Culture Change Committee**
>
> Finding answers. What is our culture now? Where should it be? What gaps need to be closed? What action needs to be taken

The next chapter explains how the culture change committee will move forward.

> # BUT I AM FRUSTRATED.
> # CAN'T WE START SOMETHING NOW?

Glad you asked. There is an approach that might allow you to get going quickly and build your foundations around specific issues.

4.5   Employees for Change Action Groups.

The idea around this is to select a specific topic that there is wide support for and start looking at that one specific issue. There are at least two current challenges facing business where action is underway – yet people are concerned that its' not happening fast enough.

Employees for climate change
Probably the most important issue today is climate change. The Responsible Business 2030 webpage talks specifically about "Employees for Climate Change Action Group." It suggests that a group of employees who

share a concern that their organisation could be doing more to help with climate change, get together and start suggesting ideas about what can be done. The suggested approach includes a pledge that individuals could sign as their commitment to work on the initiative.

Employees for Climate Action Pledge

I will actively encourage my Company (and my colleagues)
to accept its responsibility towards climate and planet issues,
to minimise its impact on the planet and
to action this as quickly as possible.

I will do this responsibly,
respecting that the company needs to make an ethical profit
and that the transition to zero carbon must be JUST, cognisant
of the needs of others on the journey.

This type of initiative is gaining momentum. In March 2023 a Canadian organisation, Climate Neutral Club, received $1.4 million in funding to help develop workforce led initiatives on climate change. This is the type of organisation that could work with your team to develop a local strategy.

Employees for equity.
One other critical area is the challenge of how people are treated in an organisation. Is it fair? Is it equitable? Is it a physically and mentally safe workplace?

When I researched the background for "Toxic Cultures" that I wrote in 2022, I was amazed that there were so many situations where organisations were being taken to court for offences against their workforce – particularly areas such as harassment.

While there are laws in place that set minimum standards in areas like hiring and employment equity, as well as "equal pay for equal work," there still seem to be too many occasions where what actually happens in the day-to-day activity inside the organisation doesn't live up to expectations. It's not socially responsible.

This is another area where management from the board level down would probably want to support any action that identifies problems and starts to put in place corrective action.

Maybe starting an "Employees for Equity" action group could be a quick start way to start things happening?

Some thought-provoking questions.

What are your thoughts and reflections on this chapter? Take some time to consider and possibly discuss with others.

The suggestion	Agree	Dis-agree	Let's Chat
Are you proud of the steps your organization is taking to address societal issues?			
Senior management will be "on board" with this initiative.			
You have a plan for communications?			
Your workplace is already PSYCHOLOGICALLY SAFE?			
The term "holistic" is familiar to you and is the way your business operates today.			
There are some who will need convincing of the need for change. (If "agree – what's the plan?)			
Are the steps to setting up a culture change committee adequate? (Can you think of more? Is there a plan)			
Have you identified other "early adopters" who can be part of the initial team?			
There will be areas of resistance. (What will be your plan for this?)			

The suggestion	Agree	Dis-agree	Let's Chat
The board and senior management will be keen to be engaged. (If disagree – what's the plan?)			
The example "commitment to change" letter will work and can be sent by the board and management to all employees? (If disagree what's the plan?)			

Step one: creating the framework

5 Step two: set goals and reality check.

Once the approval of the board and senior management has been obtained, the work of the committee ramps up. Step One in the process ensured that the necessary support for change existed at the leadership level and a clear message was sent to all employees. Step Two, "Set Goals and Reality Check" focuses on the work of the culture change committee.

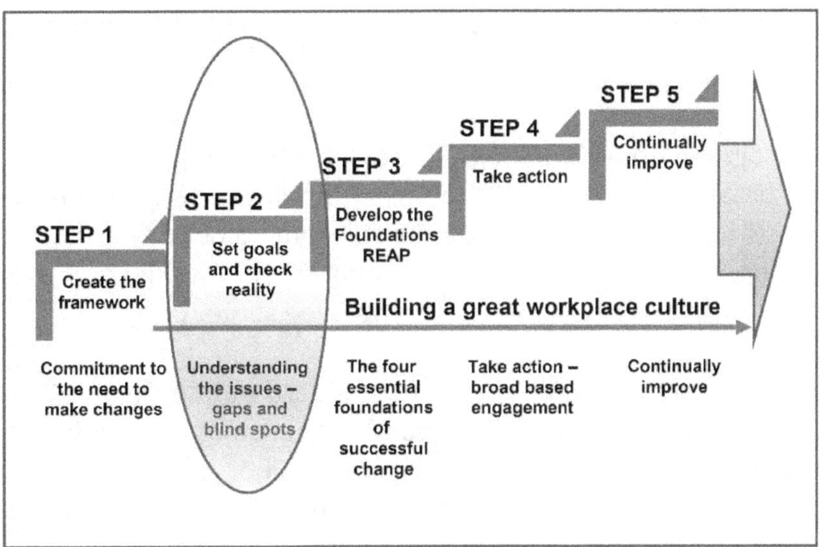

The work of the Culture Change Committee

The work of the culture change committee will provide the essential information that allows the creation of an action plan to move towards a desired state or culture. To move from "the way things are" to "a managed approach to how we want things to be."

There are four main activities in this step of the process. Defining what the "current state" is; establishing agreement on where we need to be; looking at the results to determine where the gaps (and priorities) are and finally putting an action plan in place to start closing the gap.

Where are we now?	Assessment of what the existing company culture appears to be based on reputation, action and behaviour
Where do we need to be?	Can we create a description or definition about what people see as "a responsible business" and a great place to work?
Where are the gaps?	What are the key gaps between "what is" and "what should be." Creates a basis for setting priorities
What actions are needed?	Who needs to take what action in order for things to change, ensuring that changes become "embedded?"

Where are we now? Finding the data (reality check)

Many organizations may already have employee satisfaction metrics and other statistical information that is relevant to culture. Information from exit interviews is an example. All existing sources should be used as part of data gathering. This includes past employee surveys.

Many organizations have relied on standard employee surveys as a core tool for obtaining employee feedback. We recommend that in this situation the culture change team looks at a combination of these standard survey tools with generic questions but also "engages" with a cross section of employees. (This should include all "people" aspects of the organization – including both full time employees, plus sub-contractors, agency staff and even supplier and customer employees).

Often employees are frustrated with traditional surveys citing lack of engagement, not asking the right questions, and therefore avoiding problem areas, and lack of any meaningful follow up and response by management. These barriers must be removed to obtain an honest and meaningful assessment of "reality."

Some of the questions asked should include items such as the employees' levels of happiness, mental and physical health, working conditions, engagement, fulfilment, empowerment, and responsibility.

Also needed will be the employees' views on the current company culture, leadership, fairness, pay levels, ethics, training and others. A great deal of research continues to be developed on understanding employee engagement which is strongly driven by culture.

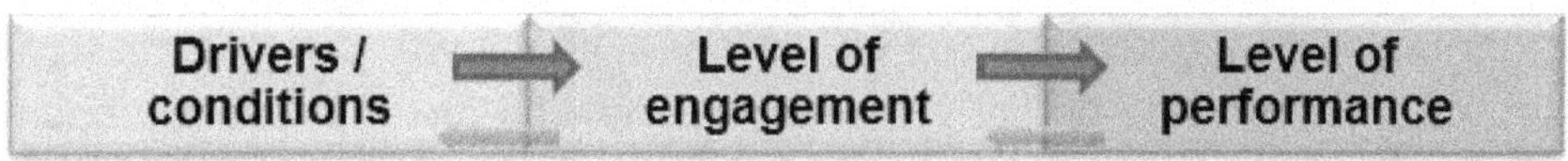

The drivers or working conditions within the workplace determine the level of employee engagement; the level of engagement then determines the level of organizational performance. Data gathering needs to find out what the drivers of engagement (and disengagement are). Research also shows that lower performance also feeds back to lower engagement – people get de-motivated and less committed; lower engagement also feeds back into an impact on the drivers. So, as the saying goes, creating a people centric work environment is a virtuous loop.

While many surveys concentrate on "systemic" drivers, things like workload, pay and compensation, training opportunities etc. they often fail to assess how people "feel they are being treated." These emotional aspects are key drivers of workplace behaviour.

Paying people well and having the best benefits in the world and providing perks like a relaxation lounge, "play" areas, free food, health clubs etc. is all wasted if people are de-motivated by not being treated well. This includes fairness, honesty, trust, opportunity and other "on the job" realities. Any data gathering for "where are we now" MUST include these aspects.

Where do we need to be?
What do people want from their work and the work environment? What do employees wish the company culture to be? Should there be a better definition of the social and business purpose of the company? Do people need to see the connection between the company purpose and the purpose of their job? Typically, these definitions of the "desired state" will break down into the aspects of "vision of a great workplace."

One area is "task" related. This is tied to the business purpose of the company. Employees need to be closely aligned with the business of the company and their activities must clearly link to the overall business direction. The often-missing area is engagement – a great work environment. A great workplace would include desirable approaches to:

- Working in a great workplace culture (where fairness, respect and well-being are prioritised).
- Knowing how "my work" fits into the big picture (purpose) – understanding what is expected of me.
- Understanding the scope and flexibility of my work
- Having the equipment needed to do my job.
- Having all the other "task support" for my job
- Working with a manageable workload
- Being able to suggest and influence ways my work can be improved.
- Receiving regular, fair, and unbiased feedback
- Receiving the training needed for my job.
- Having a "boss" who treats me fairly and as part of a "team."
- Having some level of autonomy to do my work.

- Having some fun and friendship at work.

Another area related to the workplace itself – could deal with health and safety issues – both physical and mental health. Career development and opportunities to grow and advance should also be available.

A core area related to culture, and emerging as a key driver in engagement, is looking at how individuals are treated (and treat each other) in the workplace. Clarity around these expectations will be central to the later development of organizational values. Expectations may include:

- Relationships with other workers are positive.
- Relationships where people are supportive and collaborative.
- A workplace where individuals are respected and valued.
- Trust exists in the workplace especially between employees and managers / supervisors.
- Clear communications exist (good and frequent - two ways)
- There is no discrimination of any type.
- Individuals are treated fairly in all aspects.
- The "voice of the employee" is heard, valued, and acted upon

An effective workplace would also recognize individuals as a "whole person – twenty-four hours a day, seven days a week." Individuals may feel that the workplace needs to enhance and improve its ability to hear, understand and respond to personal issues that an employee may be having that impact their work.

Creating a safe space for people to express their views and ACTIVE hearing of what they say is critical at this stage.

This data collection, discussion and debate is a critical aspect of building a "cultural framework" that forms the foundation of behaviour and decision making going forward. This process must be comprehensive in that employees need to feel engaged and valued in terms of their input, but management must also be involved as changes may be needed to policies, procedures and other existing approaches to planning, operations, measurement, and management feedback.

Asking the right questions is also critical. Allowing the data gathering to flow even if the views being expressed may be uncomfortable. Often engaging an independent facilitator may help this objectivity.

Where are the gaps?
This data gathering activity is the foundation of moving forward. The Culture Change Committee has now done the work and has discussed findings with management, who has worked with the board to obtain agreement on the "desired state / desired culture." The outcome of these discussions must be clarity of the existing gaps and their "level of pain" (impact / importance) in terms of barriers to an effective culture.

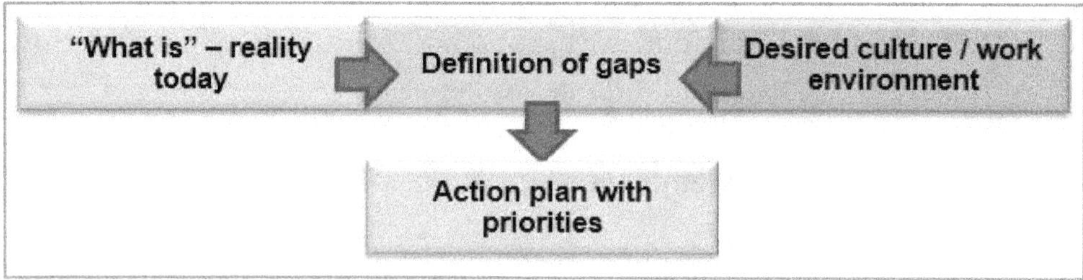

Not everything can be addressed at once, but the action plan should reflect the highest priorities which should be addressed first to "ease the pain."

These initial gaps are often referred to as "low hanging fruit" as they are selected to start demonstrating that "change is actually happening." Priorities will be organization specific and will be the result of knowing the gaps but also considering aspects such as how critical the gap is seen to be. The results may reveal:

- High levels of stress and poor mental health.

- Concerns about the company's negative impact on the environment.
- Perceived unfairness on issues such as pay, opportunities, diversity.
- Process, equipment, or work organisation problems.
- Lack of inclusion.
- Harassment, micro-aggression, discrimination.

Often the list of "gaps" and areas for improvement can be long. Where to start? What should be addressed first? Very often a point scoring system can be applied to the gaps to determine priorities.

The initial focus is not always the biggest problem or issue; often achieving "early wins" can provide support and motivation. The factors used to develop "scores" can include:

- Ease of implementation (speed, changes needed)
- Value in demonstrating "commitment to change" by management.
- Resources required.
- Breadth of the problem (location, region, department)
- Reputation and brand impact
- Impact on staff turnover and possible "hiring barriers".

Clear communication of the list of identified gaps must be made available to the employees together with a communication on steps forward. Which brings us to the action plan.

Action plan

Two approaches will be needed to close the gaps in the action plan. Corrective action and Preventative action.

In simple terms corrective action prevents recurrence, while preventative action prevents occurrence. Corrective action is carried out after a non-conformity has already occurred, whereas preventative action is planned with the goal of preventing a nonconformity in the first place.

The most important challenge is that whatever changes are made, they become embedded in the way that the organization moves forward. So many change initiatives fail because the action plan is seen as a stand-alone project. If the project is running, the changes happen – but when the project is over, the organization slips back into its old ways and the culture once again becomes "unmanaged."

Corrective action

One regular problem with organizational culture is that an organization is seen to say one thing and do another. This REALLY frustrates and de-motivates employees because action does not reflect an existing policy or procedure. This is often referred to as a "lack of alignment."

Sometimes this occurs because of poorly worded policies or procedures that are open to different interpretations. It may be because one manager chooses to implement a certain policy and another "works around it." It may also be because of poor supervisor selection and training.

Whatever the issue, the action plan will focus on *corrective action*. This includes re-writing, re-stating, re-training, re-assignment, or other actions to ensure that the desired state that is already planned, is correctly and consistently implemented. The culture change committee must assess what the root cause of the problem was and seek a real solution.

Preventative action

The second types of action are _preventative action_. These aspects will require changes to the "way we do things around here" – either because the issue or problem has never been considered or because an existing approach is clearly not delivering the desired action.

These actions are particularly important in embedding the change and will involve policy and procedural changes that will extend across the whole business. To not make these changes meets the definition of insanity.

If the goal is to have something different happen from what is reflected in the existing "reality" then something needs to be changed.

So often organizations think the solution to the required changes is to "try harder." Nothing could be further from the truth. If it's not working – is it execution or is it the wrong plan, policy, or procedure? To many employees this seems like insanity. "Management keeps telling me to do it this way, but I know it won't work."

Insanity Is Doing the Same Thing Over and Over Again and Expecting Different Results

The action plan must have support at all levels and be effectively resourced and communicated. There must be clearly defined roles, accountability, and responsibilities in the plan. Resources required, timelines, deliverables, inter-dependencies, risks, measurements, regular reviews, and contingencies are all normal plan aspects.

The Culture Change Committee must exercise major influence over what changes need to be made.

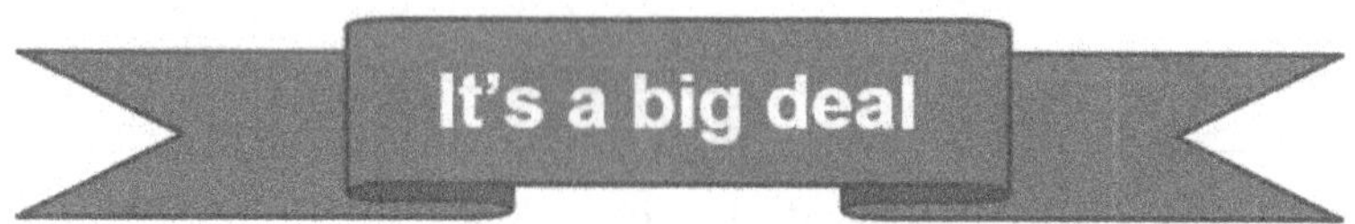

Arriving at the action plan is a <u>REALLY big deal</u>. This is the core of the changes that are needed to start becoming a responsible business. Listening to employees. Being willing to hear both good and bad news. Being willing to hear "the voice of the employee" – seeing people as partners and not just resources. Being willing to change. Putting resources into changing the way things are.

As the required changes start to be made, driven by employee engagement, ideas and suggestions, the culture itself will start to change.

In an earlier chapter we talked about the critical need to give culture an equal role in the business model – plan, do, check, and act. This is the solid first stage of planning that is leading to an action plan (the "do") to ensure that "what we say is what we do." Culture is no longer an unplanned, self-developing approach to "the way we do things around here" but a planned and managed component of the overall business model. THIS is the way we do things around here.

By the way – don't forget to continually communicate and check back to make sure things are progressing as planned. Celebrate successes. Say thanks. Demonstrate appreciation as goals are achieved. Learn from mistakes – it won't all be perfect. Be honest about mistakes – this will help develop trust. How management allows this evolution to take place will demonstrate a real commitment to change.

Change is underway. The desired culture has been developed. People are engaged. Management and the board are committed. Let's look a bit deeper into what is happening. How is the action plan building the foundations for a responsible business?

A final word. It must be starting to become clear that this is not an HR issue – it is a strategic approach to how the business is operated. HR will continue to play a key role – but the effectiveness of any workplace culture ultimately depends on great leadership as at levels. (Don't ask HR to "fix the culture problem!")

Some thought-provoking questions.

What are your thoughts and reflections on this chapter? Take some time to consider and possibly discuss with others.

The suggestion	Agree	Dis-agree	Let's Chat
You already have data on your culture. (If disagree what's the plan?)			
You have identified approaches to additional data gathering.			
You have a clear idea on how to obtain involvement in data gathering.			
There are "nonemployees" who should also be included in data gathering.			
Are some of the ideas of "a great workplace culture" applicable to you?			
You have a plan on how to develop a great workplace for your organisation.			
You have determined how you will set priorities from among the many ideas.			
You have a plan on how management and workforce ideas will be integrated and reconciled.			

The suggestion	Agree	Dis-agree	Let's Chat
Many of your issues are non-compliance (I.e., you already have the policies in place, but they are being ignored).			
Many of your issues need preventative action. New policies need to be developed and agreed.			

6 Step three: develop the foundations.

Step Three will take the output from the work of the Culture Change Committee and put it into action.

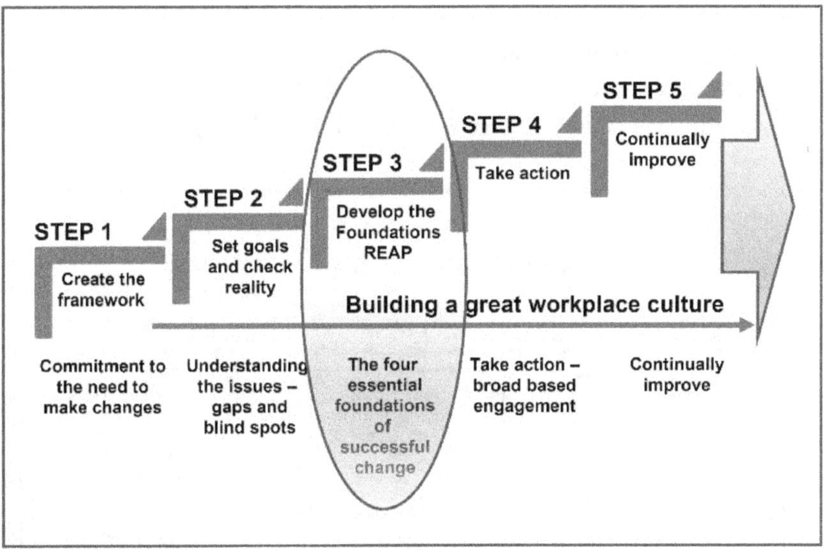

This will require developing the four major foundation stones of a great workplace culture - these being:

- **RESPONSIBILITY**: an environment where responsible decision-making predominates,
- **ETHICS**: agreeing the core corporate values and a company code of ethics,

Step three: develop the foundations.

- **ACTION**; placing emphasis on the importance of action, and,
- **PURPOSE**: developing the Company's social purpose – why the company exists, in what way does it benefit society.

This stage is part of the action plan itself. The acronym REAP is used because there are four essential "foundations" that will need to be addressed. These foundations are the factors that support the three pillars of a responsible business. While they are presented as guidelines, it should become clear that they provide a solid foundation for a planned and managed culture upon which a responsible business rests.

6.1   Pillars and foundations

The pillars of responsible business

Earlier in the book we introduced the pillars of a responsible business – people, planet, and profit. Holding this up, are the foundations.

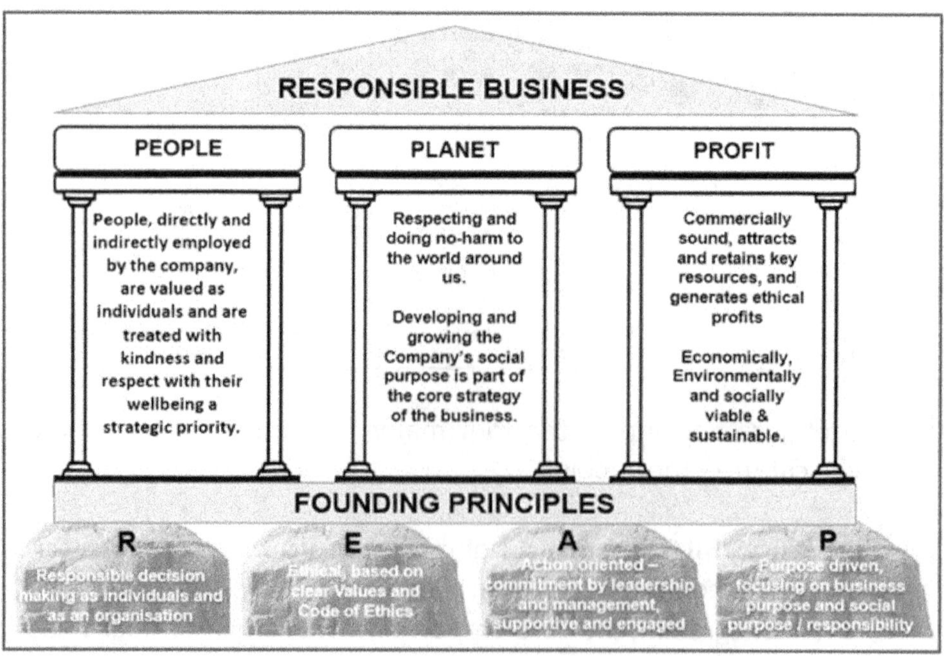

Step three: develop the foundations.

People, Planet and Profit is not a new idea – having been first suggested by Ben & Jerry's Ice Cream, at a time when they were a leader in progressive corporate thinking and prior to them being acquired by the giant Unilever. (A potentially great fit as Paul Polman, the retired CEO of Unilever continues to be an activist for responsible business). John Elkington the founder of AA1000 was also an early promoter of People, Planet and Profit.

While many new slogans and ideas have developed since then, these three pillars have stood the test of time and remain central to building a responsible business. However, these pillars must be built on foundations – and it is these foundations that need to be established as part of step three in the process.

The foundations of a responsible business
An organization can only be responsible if those within it act responsibly and make responsible decisions. That's it. Not complex – everything rests on behaviour. Each of four components has a major impact on how an organization is run and how it behaves.

> **Responsible people + Responsible decision making = Responsible organization**

REAP is an acronym for the four key aspects of the foundation for a responsible business.

R	Responsible decision making
E	Ethics and values
A	Action by leadership
P	Purpose within society

Step three: develop the foundations.

If a business wants to be seen to act responsibly, then that is "how things must be done." Each aspect of REAP is interdependent and together these four areas build a cultural and behavioural framework.

"Surprises" and irresponsible decisions can occur in any organization. Having a defined and shared foundation in place will ensure that clear expectations of acceptable behaviour are established, and irresponsible behaviour and decisions are less likely. Risks are reduced.

REAP – the four foundation stones.

The four aspects of REAP are shown in chart below. These are then discussed in detail.

<table>
<tr><td>RESPONSIBLE DECISION MAKING

Being accountable and taking ownership for personal and organizational decisions.
A workplace where responsible decision-making is commonplace</td><td>ETHICS AND VALUES

Values and the Code of Ethics that drive decision making in the company.

Ethical training is vital – developing "ethical" muscle</td></tr>
<tr><td>ACTION FOR LEADERSHIP

Commitment and action from management to take the lead

• Governance framework for responsible action / accountability
• A holistic and sustained strategy for a great workplace culture
• Being good role models
• Engage everyone in the process
• Providing financial support and time
• Actively supporting change-makers</td><td>PURPOSE IN SOCIETY

• To be a Responsible Business
• To serve and support society
• To respect the environment, and
• To make an ethical profit</td></tr>
</table>

6.2   Responsible decision making

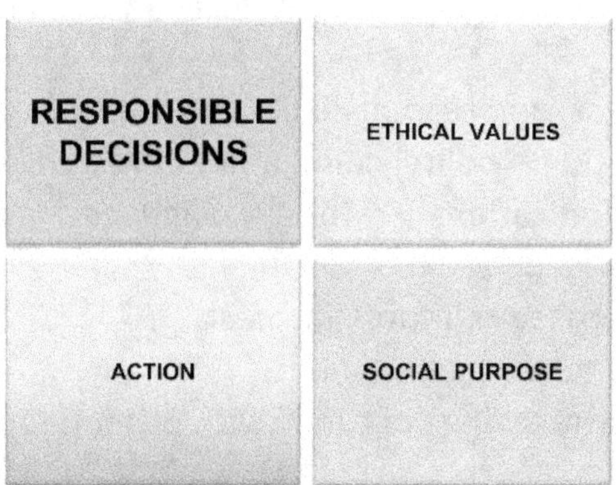

Responsible decision-making has been defined as "the ability to make caring and constructive choices about personal behaviour and social interactions across diverse situations. This includes the capacities to consider ethical standards and safety concerns, and to evaluate the benefits and consequences of various actions for personal, social, and collective well-being."

Individual decisions are what drive organizational behaviour – an organization may have a legal identity, but organisational behaviour is a reflection of individual and collective behaviour. This means "it starts with

#ItStartsWithMe	**Hold the mirror up. Responsible behaviour starts with me. Personal accountability.**

me."

Organizational change cannot take place unless it starts with individuals making different decisions. So why "Responsible Decision Making?

Responsible Decision Making	**Because decision making by individuals is the foundation of organizational behaviour and drives a responsible business. It impacts all relationships as well as work performance.**

As individuals, we alone decide how we behave towards others; our actions are the foundations upon which relationships are built. Positive relationships are essential for a healthy and productive workplace. In this area responsibility includes:

- Responsibility towards oneself – mental, physical, and financial wellness.
- Respect, compassion, fairness, and responsibility towards others.
- Effective verbal communication – polite, calm, and interested.
- Effective nonverbal communications – "body language," facial expressions, posture, voice.
- Listening and questioning – these reinforce interest.
- Manners – vital with different cultures.
- Social awareness and empathy, being "in tune" with other people's emotions.
- Self-management – controlling our own emotions.
- Humble confidence.

All the above can be learnt by developing awareness and training and have a bearing on how we treat others. Most importantly, they determine we are perceived by others. A key challenge relating to effective inter-personal relationships is the impact of different personalities and the human tendency to "react" to the actions of other people rather to manage our own actions.

A responsible business understands the complexity of human behaviour and embraces tools, training programmes and approaches that help improve the probability of predictable and responsible behaviour.

We also have a responsibility to ensure that prior to making a decision we think about the possible implications and unintended consequences of the decision. Individual action will determine whether decisions are seen as responsible. As an individual each person needs:

- To treat ourselves, colleagues, others, society, and the environment fairly and with respect, compassion, and love and kindness.

Step three: develop the foundations.

- To help build (or maintain) a workplace culture, within our sphere of influence, where we and our colleagues return home from work happy and healthy to enjoy life outside of the workplace.
- To endeavour never to do anything illegal or unethical or ask a colleague to do anything illegal or unethical and encourage others to do likewise, with our decisions meeting the requirements of the company's social and environmental purpose.
- To make decisions, both personal and corporate, that accord with the Company's values and Code of Ethics.

It is a challenge for individuals to "manage" their behaviours unless they have a degree of self-awareness. This is one of the benefits of approaches such as team development, which is particularly important when it relates to decision making by those in leadership positions. The work climate can also affect decision making – whether we feel positive or negative.

> *"Optimism is a strategy for making a better future. Because unless you believe that the future can be better, you are unlikely to step up and take responsibility for making it so."*
>
> — *Noam Chomsky.*

Responsibility goes beyond legal requirements.
Most organizations provide policies and procedures that are supposed to guide decision making. These are quite rightly based on legal requirements – it is vital that employees have an understanding of the law.

But most decisions cannot be covered by pre-defined instructions. This has been referred to as "managing in the white space." What do people do where there is no guidance? What happens when the guidance seems inconsistent with what a person believes to be fair, right, and responsible?

Decisions are made explicitly through consciously combining personal beliefs and values to choose a course of action. If an individual feels or knows that their own values and beliefs are consistent with, supported by and will be endorsed by their organisation, then there should be no fear about making a decision. This is often defined within a code of conduct or similar statement. This brings us to the next of the four foundations.

6.3   Ethics and values

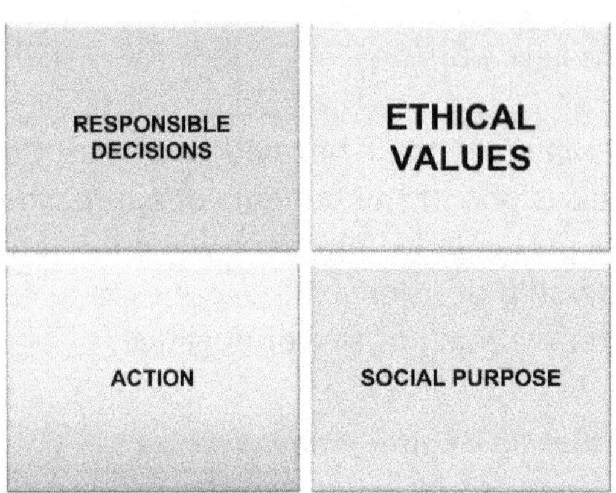

Business must operate both within the frameworks of law and within socially accepted norms of behaviour. This is closely tied to being a responsible business – if an organization fails to act in a way that is seen by others as responsible then, by definition, it risks acting irresponsibly.

Every individual who makes a decision will be guided by their own personal belief, values, and code of ethics. Organisations face considerable risk if there is no dialogue or agreement around how individual decision making may fit with an organisation's expectations. (Individual and collective values).

Ethics and Values	Unless an organization provides guidance on expected behaviour, individuals may act "as they see fit." This increases the risk of and being seen to act irresponsibly.

A more detailed discussion on ethics and values is contained in the chapter on developing a code of ethics. (Chapter 10 Guidance - creating a Code of Ethics).

Step three: develop the foundations.

At this point we focus on the core need to put in place a code that reflects a mutually agreed foundation for behaviour within the organisation.

A company Code of Ethics is essential.

A shared commitment to a set of values, together with a Code of Ethics will help guide decision making.

Decisions are made explicitly whenever one consciously combines beliefs and values in order to choose a course of action. They are made implicitly whenever one relies on a ritualized response (habit, tradition) to cope with a choice between options. Repetition of past decisions may result in suboptimal choices; however, it may also provide a ready escape from the difficulties and expense of explicit decision making

Research Needs for Human Factors. Washington, DC: The National Academies Press.

In "responsible decision making" each decision should be "thought about." That is what explicit means. However, often decisions are implicit – made more by ritual than the conscious thought, required for responsible decisions.

Decision making combines ethics and values. While ethics tend to be consistent within a society, values are different for different persons, i.e., what is important for one person, may not be important for another person. Values tell us what we want to do or achieve in our life, whereas ethics helps us in deciding what is morally correct or incorrect, in the given situation.

Personal Values can be defined as:

- The principles and standards upon which we lead our lives.
- Our beliefs that come from our background, education, and our individual and wider social networks – in essence our "worldview."

Step three: develop the foundations.

- Personal ideas and beliefs, that can originate from prejudice, myths, and assumptions.

But surely as long as a business adheres to the law, ethics is a "nice to have" unless it gets in the way of us being competitive?

Typically, a Code of Ethics will include a statement relating to a commitment to abide by the law. However, what a Code's main purpose will be is to document specific areas where there is no LEGAL requirement to behave in a certain way, but there is a **moral and social responsibility** to do so.

Thus, a Code of Ethics should inform people of the expected foundations of behaviour and decision making "in the white spaces." The code will fill the gap between what is defined by acting within the law and what is expected as "socially acceptable" behaviour.

The challenge is defining expectations of behaviour that should be built into a code of ethics.

A great example of the importance of this guidance in behaviour and decision-making is behind the expression "moments of truth."

There will be many situations where an individual working for an organization is in a "one on one" interaction with another employee, a customer, a supplier or in fact anyone. Especially true between supervisors / managers and others.

How this person acts and behaves at this point will be a moment of truth because it will demonstrate the values and ethics that the organization appears to represent.

If the person has no guidance on what is expected or reacts, not thinking of the underlying consequences – they may resort to an implicit, ritualized response. "Sorry, that's company policy" – ignoring and not addressing the concerns of the customer.

This is particularly important when applied to guiding decisions made by leaders and managers. If there is not a common and shared set of expectations around behaviour, then inconsistency and conflicts can easily occur.

It is also a problem when an individual's set of personal values conflict with the shared values of the organization they work for. This is a major cause of both personal stress and individual frustration and demotivation.

Developing a Code of Ethics can be a challenging activity. There will be many ideas and opinions. What are values? How do Values affect Ethics? Do we need a Code of Ethics or a Code of Conduct? Which values are "right" and should be used?

As a reminder, to help in this process as well as provide examples we have added "guidance" in chapter 10, on developing a Code of Ethics that provides support materials as well as some examples.

6.4   Action by leadership

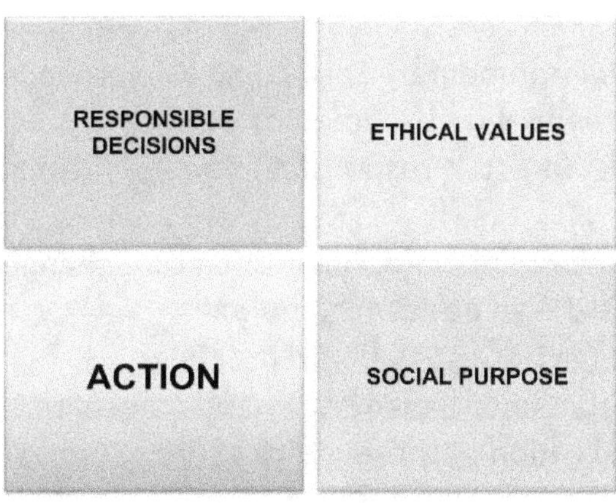

Action by leadership, especially behaviour and decision making, must be consistent with the desire to build a responsible business.

It should start with the Board. Then all levels of management, from "C" suite / Director level throughout the organisation to the role of direct supervisors.

Leaders will "set the tone."

There are many situations where action by leaders acts as a foundation for a responsible business. First at the highest level — where the board is responsible for governance.

Action by Leadership	Leadership "sets the tone" as to how the business will be managed. Leaders are responsible for all aspects of the business model - planning, execution, monitoring and action

We have already discussed how the board must be behind the initial activities of support the Culture Change Committee — but the boards involvement must be permanent. The boards decision making must be seen as consistent and supportive of the desired culture.

Ongoing boardroom support

Board level commitment to a great workplace culture is critical to being a responsible business. Championing and driving an ongoing holistic strategy that provides sufficient time, budget, and resources to make it happen with:

- an understanding that we all have a responsibility to make ethical decisions.
- a public commitment to Environmental, Social and Governance (ESG) issues in Annual Statement and other media.
- a director or Non-Executive Director responsible for monitoring boardroom ethics.
- the appointment of someone with responsibility for culture change with direct access to the board — an ethics "champion"
- workplace culture as an agenda Item at all board meetings.
- continual monitoring of people and planet issues and transparent (honest) promotion and publication of these metrics.

Step three: develop the foundations.

- the provision of an adequate training budget – both money and time – with a strong focus on prevention.

Leadership action is critical at every step of planning, execution, monitoring, and decision making. This is further explained as part of the business model outlined in Chapter 11. This explains how the PDCA (Plan, Do, Check, and Act) approach to a business model integrates with the five-step approach.

At the "planning" stage, equal attention is given to both task (what we want to achieve) and the behaviour. What we do and how we will behave doing it.

At the "do" or operational execution stage, leaders must focus on both *management of processes and behaviours equally*.

The "checking" stage, measurement and feedback must be holistic covering both operational performance as well as work climate / culture and consistency of behaviours.

Finally, the "act" stage. Management must take action to respond to problems and issues. How leaders behave every time they make a decision and take action will either reinforce or detract from the goal of being seen as a responsible business.

Leadership really does set an example; leaders should ensure that inter-actions among others are positive and should coach others in situations where there appears to be a lack of alignment with the values and ethics. Leaders are responsible for setting an example based on expected behaviours. They also monitor individual and inter-personal behaviour within the organization and are accountable to ensure that reality reflects intention. Leaders make a responsible business an operational reality.

6.5   Purpose driven.

While "business purpose" has traditionally been part of strategic thinking, today "social purpose" in terms of the responsibility of business as a member of society must also be included.

When a business is established, it is recognized as an independent entity, with responsibilities, rights, and obligations. The phrase "license to operate" is often used as an expression of the accountability that a business accepts when it is recognized as a legal entity.

Purpose driven	The purpose of a business has a duality. Its' business purpose as well as its social purpose and responsibility as a member of society.

In exchange for this recognition as a legal entity, society has expectations of how a business, as a member of society, is expected to operate and behave. Citizens are required to act responsibly. So are organizations. Business Purpose therefore includes both the reason a business was established and equally the responsibility it takes on as a "corporate citizen."

Business Round Table Statement of Purpose.
In recent years public and regulatory pressure has led to many organisations redefining their purpose. This shift aims to move from shareholders as the driver of business purpose, to the broader based stakeholder approach.

Step three: develop the foundations.

The following statement supports and reinforces this shift in focus of business purpose to a broader perspective.

In 2019, the US based Business Roundtable announced the release of a new <u>Statement on the Purpose of a Corporation</u> signed by 181 CEOs who commit to lead their companies for the benefit of all stakeholders – customers, employees, suppliers, communities and shareholders.

Since 1978, Business Roundtable has periodically issued Principles of Corporate Governance. Each version of the document issued since 1997 has endorsed principles of shareholder primacy – that corporations exist principally to serve shareholders. With today's announcement, the new Statement supersedes previous statements and outlines a modern standard for corporate responsibility.

This shift is reflected by several public statements made by individual leaders of major organisations. The following quotes are a mixture of business purpose (usually "to make a profit" – the commercial objective) and social purpose – to serve society and respect the planet.

"Society is demanding that companies, both public and private, serve a social purpose. Purpose unifies management, employees, and communities. It drives ethical behaviour and creates an essential check on actions that go against the best interests of stakeholders. Purpose guides culture, provides a framework for consistent decision-making, and, ultimately, helps sustain long-term financial returns for the shareholders of your company."

Larry Fink, CEO of BlackRock Asset Management, January 2019 letter to CEOs.

"Employees with a shared sense of purpose not only find more meaning in their work but are willing to give more discretionary effort and are also more satisfied with their pay".

CIPD, Chartered Institute of Personnel and Development UK)

Step three: develop the foundations.

"Businesses cannot survive without profits, just like my body can't survive without producing red blood cells, but my purpose is not to produce red blood cells.".

Quote by 2013 interview with John Mackey, the founding CEO of Whole Foods, by Robert Reiss published in Forbes.

Corporate purpose is "producing profitable solutions for the problems of the people and planet, and not profiting from creating problems".

Definition by Colin Mayer4 Peter Moores Professor of Management Studies at the Saïd Business School at the University of Oxford (This definition has been adopted by the World Economic Forum (WEF), the Enacting Purpose Initiative and the British Academy, among other prominent organisations).

For purpose to mean more than words, it has to become an organising principle for organisations and their leadership teams. Purpose, well defined, becomes a 'north star', informing the strategic choices faced by the board and its senior management team.

From "Enacting Purpose Initiative, 2020," Saïd Business School, Oxford

"Almost 9 in 10 employees believe that the "success of a business" should be measured in terms of more than just its financial performance".

and

"60% of millennials want to join companies with a "purpose" embedded in the business".

Deloitte's Millennial Survey

Social Purpose

Business texts are full of information about traditional statements of purpose – "what is the business in business to do," but what is SOCIAL purpose? Social Purpose is about:

- What the company really stands for, its *core reason for being* and why it exists outside of just making a profit.
- *Its' higher purpose*, and reason be being, above just profit. Where it can make a unique and positive impact.
- Focusing the company, and its people, on what is most important and where it can create the greatest value.
- Why the world is a better place because of the existence of the company.

Being a socially responsible company is a requirement for the "license to operate." This secures the trust of society, the local community, and other stakeholders, providing advocacy, legitimacy, and approval for the business rather than just acceptance or even worse rejection. Establishing social purpose should be a part, albeit a vital part, of a holistic strategy to create a great workplace culture.

Why is *social purpose* the new mantra for business? (The term is not used in the sense of the emerging social purpose corporations in the USA but how a business makes a positive economic, social, and environmental impact in the world).

Moral and responsible reasons

- Without the existence of a stable, civil society, there would be no educated and diligent employees and no effective infrastructure such as hospitals, welfare, law and order, transport, and power.
- Business has a moral and legal duty to repay society for using the services provided by government and civil society.
- Staff are more likely to be happy in their job, healthier and more motivated in a purpose driven organisation.

Step three: develop the foundations.

Practical reasons
- 60% of millennials want to join companies with a "purpose" that is embedded in the business – strong corporate social purpose attracts and retains top talent which in turn reduces costs.
- Reduces staff turnover and enhances "engagement."
- Mitigates risk of scandals and prosecution (including the defence of having awareness and having taken action).
  - Reduces absenteeism and presenteeism.
  - Has a positive impact on:
    - brand image – customer perception
    - teamwork, engagement, creativity, happiness, morale
    - physical and mental health – wellbeing
    - productivity
- Reduction in risk associated with the effective operation of the business model, especially related to "human capital."

"Business in Society" reasons
- Reinforces the social license of business within society.
- Enables the linkage between business capability and societal needs such as addressing climate change.
- Responds to perceptions that business "focuses only on making money."
- Addresses perceptions (and reality) that the workplace contributes to negative societal issues such as increasing mental health problems.
- Address irritants caused by perception (and sometimes reality) of irresponsible behaviour, such as unethical decisions, manipulation of legal requirements including tax issues.

Social Purpose must drive an organization's decision-making process in much the same way that ethics and values are considered. It is often a challenge to figure out what social purpose really means.

Here are some possible questions that people can be asked about social purpose, designed to get a feel of the level of understanding of the company's existing social purpose, how well it is communicated and whether it meets with employee expectations. These questions can be included in the work of the Culture Change Committee as well as becoming part of an anonymous, annual employee survey.

1. **Are you aware of the company's social purpose?**
2. **Do you feel the company's social purpose is clearly articulated?**
3. **Do you feel it is embedded into the DNA of the company?**
4. **Do you feel the company's social purpose is considered when decisions are being made?**
5. **Do you feel that the Directors behaviour and decision-making is in line with the company's social purpose?**
6. **Do you feel that your managers behaviour and decision-making is in line with the company's social purpose?**
7. **To what extent do you feel your friends and family are aware of the company's social purpose.**
8. **Do you feel proud of working for the company.**
9. **Do you believe the company contributes to resolving some of society's problems or make them worse?**
10. **Do you believe the company contributes to resolving the world's environmental problems or make them worse?**

The results of the survey will indicate whether all is well regards to purpose, whether the purpose needs greater communication or whether a new start is needed.

People may also be aware of the societal changes taking place such as the United Nation's SDG's or Social Development Goals that almost the entire world, through its national governments have signed up to support.

You may wish to ask employees which of the United Nations Sustainability Goals the company should prioritise maybe asking them to choose their top five priorities. A summary of these goals is contained in Chapter 9.

Step three: develop the foundations.

Some thought-provoking questions.

What are your thoughts and reflections on this chapter? Take some time to consider and discuss with others.

Thinking about these questions

The suggestion	Yes	Maybe	No
Will focusing on REAP address the main implementation issues?			
Is there consensus on the meaning of People, Planet, and Profit? (The Pillars).			
Are the foundations or founding principles, (REAP) logical supports for the Pillars?			
Will responsible decision-making help lead to a responsible business?			
Are current approaches to decision making working effectively?			
Does current decision making reflect the responsible behaviours outline (self / others)			
Do people in your organisation have adequate "self-awareness" of their own behaviour?			
Is there a code of ethics in your organisation?			
Was the Code of Ethics developed with employee input?			

The suggestion	Yes	Maybe	No
Does the organisation live its values day-to-day?			
Do the organisation's values reflect and support your own values?			
Are the organisation's values "lived and demonstrated" in leadership actions?			
Are the organisation's values positive and clearly demonstrated with 3rd parties?			
Is there adequate accountability to ensure leadership actions align with desired behaviour?			
Is sustaining the desired culture a regular board agenda and reporting item?			
Are values and ethics given equal weight to planning and managing "the work?"			
Is the organisations culture an integrated part of the business model?			
Has the business defined its purpose BOTH commercially and socially?			
Is sustaining the desired culture embedded into regular assessments, checks and reporting?			

Step three: develop the foundations.

Step three: develop the foundations.

7 Step four: action the plan

7.1   Action the Plan

A phrase springs to mind – "Just do it." Previous chapters have discussed the strategic focus of People, Planet and Profit, plus four foundations to make sure that decision making, and behaviour are consistent with expectations. Step Four in the process is getting out there and making it happen.

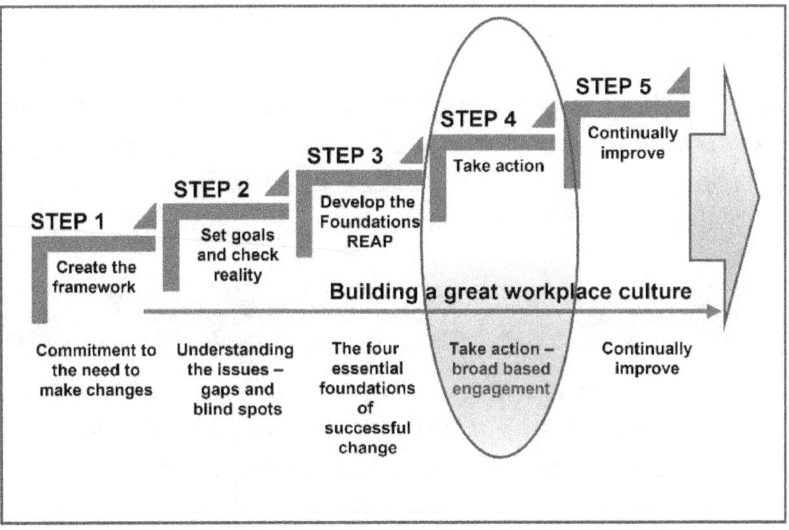

Most leaders either believe that they already run a responsible business or think that plans are in place to make it happen. However, the toughest challenge is to close the gap between one's intent to do something and actually making it happen. Step four in the plan is designed to help "operationalize" the intent to become and remain a responsible business. What can go wrong?

- The culture change initiative is seen as a project; once it ends things go back to "normal" – the way they were.
- Employees become fired up, convinced things will change but leaders fail to behave in a way that brings the desired reality "to life."
- Size becomes the enemy; CEO's believe things are changing but are too far removed from the front lines to know it's not happening.
- Staff turnover, especially at leadership levels gradually dilutes the changes and the commitments start to dissolve.
- Pressures of business build and leaders fall back into the old ways of "command and control."
- Changes in society continue but the organization is unable to keep pace with the required changes.

There are some key factors for successful culture change such as leadership buy-in, an employee centric approach and fair and transparent governance of the company. The importance of continual and transparent communication and effective training is also emphasised.

Two Quotes from Nelson Mandela

"Action without vision is only passing time,
vision without action is merely daydreaming,
but vision with action can change the world".

"We can change the world and make it a better place. It
is in your hands to make a difference."

7.2   Creating a sustained and holistic strategy.

The real key to a successful culture change initiative is that it becomes a new "way of doing things." It must become embedded in all aspects of an organization's activity. It must be part of a sustained and holistic strategy. (This is further discussed as part of integrating into the management model of plan, do, check, and act, in Chapter 11). The following are suggestions for actions that will help embed the changes.

Great leadership and management
- Continued Board support, morally and financially.
- Training for leadership and managers with emphasis on the vision (for culture change), key roles and responsibilities.
- Walking the Talk – everybody but especially leaders.
- Achieving and maintaining a great culture must be part of line managers' responsibilities and included in performance appraisals and the reward and incentive structure.

Everyone involved – people-centric.
- Ensure everyone is engaged in the culture change initiative.
- Ensure everyone sees and understand their contribution to the strategies success.
- All employees should be given mutually agreed and clearly defined responsibilities, with goals and targets with these goals factored into reviews.

Procedural alignment
- Review and update all policies to ensure that "task" oriented directives are consistent with the values and code of ethics.
- Review and update all operational procedures to ensure that they align with, complement, and support stated values and code of ethics.
- Review all compensation plans to ensure they are fair, consistent and reflect ethical commitment to fair and reasonable treatment.

Step four: action the plan.

- Review all incentive plans to ensure they include group gain sharing as well as including individual contributions.
- Review all incentive plans – especially individual ones, to ensure that there are no negative unplanned side effects. (e.g., de-motivation of group members).
- Review all leadership compensation approaches to ensure behaviour is assessed as equally important to task outcomes.
- Review all approaches to hiring and promotion to ensure that potential candidates can support and demonstrate desired values and codes of ethics.
- Enhance orientation approaches and development programs to ensure behavioural issues are included.

General
- Continual communication with all stakeholders about responsible decision-making and your great workplace culture.
- Continual measurement of metrics against targets with results published (see Chapter 12 for discussion on metrics).
- Best practices identified and continually shared and aspired to.
- Sustain an atmosphere of psychological safety where people feel safe to voice their opinion and feel able to speak-up where necessary.
- Go for some early success stories.
- Incentivise and reward success.

These suggestions can help ensure that the desired shift towards a balanced task and behaviour approach are embedded. Through this, an organizations' way of operating its' business should start to align with "responsibility."

Step four: action the plan.

7.3   Culture Change Committee ongoing role

Sustaining the activity of the culture change committee is an important step in ensuring continuity and continual improvement. A core set of individuals with in-depth experience of how the discussions around change took place can be a valuable resource moving forward. Activities might include:

- Follow up action on the priorities established in the culture gap exercise.
- Encourage more "Champions for Change" to continue to be involved.
- Report back to main board on progress. Ensure continued moral and financial support from the Board.
- Continue to involve everyone through consultation and focus groups via a fair and transparent process. Encourage buy-in to the Culture Change Initiative – a people-centric approach.
- Reemphasise, to all stakeholders, the aims of the Initiative, the survey results and planned actions going forward.
- Report success (or failure!) of activities against targets to the Board, employees, and other stakeholders. Publish a report even when the results may be disappointing. Also, no sugar coating (green washing) the results (see Metrics Chapter 12). Such transparency builds trust in management, a vital aspect of any cultural change.
- Continue with annual staff engagement surveys supported by more frequent, shorter pulse surveys. (UK Happiness Index and others).
- Continue to develop, clarify, and improve the Company Values and Code of Ethics to ensure it remains valid and realistic.

The Culture Change Committee (or re-named culture committee or whatever is chosen), might also continue to function as the focal point for the "voice of the employee." The group might work on developing processes that ensure problems and issues are raised and dealt with – such as supporting a problem identification and (speedy) resolution process, as well as a more traditional whistle blowing approach.

7.4   Fair and transparent governance

It is important to review and update policies and procedures to ensure they align with the organizations desired culture on a continuing basis. While ultimately management and the board will set policy, employee engagement will be critical to ensure buy-in – especially where problems relating to specific areas were raised by the initial work of the culture change team. Too often procedures "get in the way" of the desired behaviours.

Many of these issues will link directly to strategy; in many cases traditional decision making historically will have been focused on financial optimization, but future approaches will need to be more balanced. While cost control and containment will always be an organizational priority, the way it is achieved must reflect its' impact on all aspects and stakeholders of the business.

Some of these issues may be traditional HR policy areas, but new approaches to corporate governance require that the board is the ultimate custodian of the culture.

Many boards have compensation committees, but their work traditionally focuses on CEO and senior executive compensation only. Future approaches should have the board expanding the governance and oversight of a compensation committee, to how all compensation is strategically planned.

Increasingly, with the arrival of social media, greater regulation, and shareholder and employee activism, a poor culture can have significant adverse consequences. The risk here can be reduced by having a Culture, Risk and Compliance Committee focusing on such issues which might include:

- Pay – fair, competitive, and market-based.

- Working hours and overtime
- Contract of employment – including zero hours contracts
- Diversity and Inclusion
- Recruitment and induction
- Employee review procedures
- Equal opportunity – no discrimination
- Incentives, bonus, and benefits
- Employee Assistance Programmes
- Speak-up (voice of the employee) and whistleblowing.
- Training – particularly management / leadership aspects
- Mental, physical, and financial health – employee wellbeing
- Holiday entitlement
- Grievance procedures
- Flexible working
- Ethical supply chain
- Good jobs – training, advancement opportunities

The results of the employee survey may indicate that (some of) current processes are not considered fair and transparent. It is vital that all internal processes are fair and transparent and are also **seen** to be, as far as possible. Action may need to be taken to remedy the situation.

The company's Governing Body must be confident of receiving accurate and up-to-date information on a regular basis on how the company is run (with any material trends) enabling them to see risks and opportunities going forward. These must be balanced between task and behaviour – in effect "total system performance."

Compliance – legal and discretionary

All corporate governance frameworks are built around ensuring oversight relative to the investors and other stakeholders' interests. Traditionally this has focused heavily on investors and on *legal compliance* – directors can be held personally liable for illegal activity, which tends to ensure their attention. Future governance must embrace both legal as well as "discretionary" compliance. Those areas that define the culture and support the brand.

Legal compliance
The following are areas where the board must be aware of their legal obligations and their legal rights. legal compliance is foundational for an effective culture and will be a major irritant and de-motivator where employees know what the law is, but the organization seems to be either avoiding compliance of trying to work around its intent.

- Employment Law
- Health and Safety act 2010
- Insurance
- Fire and safety
- Human Rights issues
- Diversity and equality
- Equal opportunities
- Data protection
- Competition law
- Environmental law
- Grievance handling

In most well run (and responsible) companies many of these legal requirements will already be in place. However, there is a second area of compliance that is often not managed at the same level as legal liability yet in terms of culture should be given a prominent level of board attention.

Discretionary compliance
Control systems to manage risk are an important part of the boards responsibility with legal compliance forming a major foundation of the required controls.

Step four: action the plan.

However, there are many parts of an organizations brand and reputation and "traditions and the way of doing things" that may not require legal compliance but where an absence of governance attention, or management attention can create unwanted surprises – often leading to some level of negative financial impact.

For many organisations protection of their brand and reputation is as much about the quality of its products and services as it is about organisational behaviour as it relates to areas such as climate change, discrimination, bullying, abuse of power, unethical tax practices and many others. "Protecting the brand" in a responsible business requires high level understanding, risk management and above all ethical and honest behaviour. The governance model must address these "new" risks.

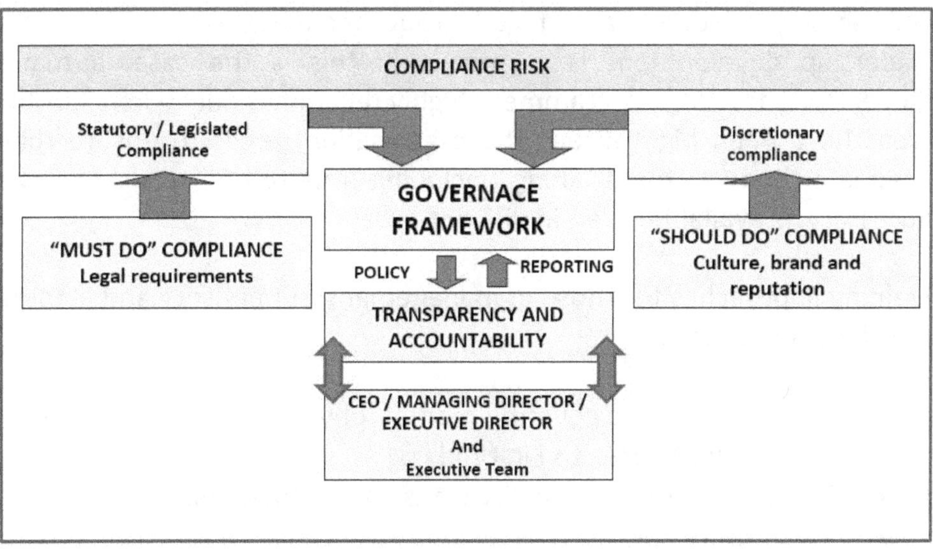

When a board is designing the systems, methods, and approaches through which it exercises its responsibility, it must address BOTH legal and discretionary compliance.

Step four: action the plan.

This means that certain attributes of the way in which an organisation is run – "the way we do things around here" may not be LEGALLY required but are just as important for understanding, measuring, supporting, and sustaining its operations. In fact, if the board REALLY understands the impact of culture it will want to provide oversight at the same level as legally required compliance.

The majority of this book has focused on what needs to be in place to build a responsible business – the strategic pillars and the four foundations (REAP) in particular. The board and senior management need to also consider what aspects of the feedback and reporting systems, necessary to ensure *discretionary compliance* are put in place.

7.5   Training Programme

The employee survey and focus group feedback could indicate that leadership development is a priority. If this is the case, a manager /supervisory training programme is highly recommended, when "problem" areas have been highlighted. The organisation needs to ensure that an adequate budget for training including one-to-one coaching where necessary, is available, even in difficult times.

Training approaches for those in management, supervisory and leadership positions should cover:

- Well-being issues covering mental, physical, and financial health – maybe Mental Health First Aid
- Self-awareness, personality traits and behaviours.
- Stress reduction
- Ethics training and developing the "ethics" muscle.
- Stigma of mental health issues
- Resilience
- How to reduce the company impact on the environment

Step four: action the plan.

- Ensuring a "whole life" approach to workload and management. (Often called work / life balance).
- How to develop a psychological safe space for speaking-up
- Life skills
- Leadership skills
- Teamwork and collaboration

The importance of these skills for middle management cannot be underestimated. Middle managers are those who have one-on-one relationships with employees, that can make or break a culture change programme.

Team Builder Leadership

Surveys suggest that drivers of job satisfaction for employees depend on interpersonal relationships they have with others, particularly management. With regards to job satisfaction, 75% of employees said the most stressful part of their job was their immediate boss. (As reported by McKinsey).

Successful team development can only take place against the backdrop of a great workplace culture, a culture based on the company Code of Ethics, its corporate values and social purpose. This also includes "great jobs" strategy, good governance, fair processes towards pay and rewards, and equality of opportunity and training.

Essential requirements for an effective team builder working at any level in the organisation includes:

- Prioritise the well-being (good mental and physical health) of her team members by investing time in social capital such as compassion, respect, empathy and encouragement combined with listening skills i.e., understanding each team member as an individual – his/her goals, interests, priorities. Set an example by prioritising your own mental and physical well-being.

Step four: action the plan.

- Co-create with them, the team's common purpose, agreeing clear and measurable goals with decisions based on the company's Code of Ethics and corporate values. Make the job rewarding, joyful and fun.
- Build trust by being credible, dependable, stable, and consistent. Be humble and accept you are certainly not the best at everything – maybe anything except being a great team leader. Be a great "role model." Understand that this can take time.
- Express (honest) gratitude for good work and celebrate success.
- Build a psychologically safe space where diverse opinions can be freely aired. The best ideas and solutions can come from surprising places. Encourage differing viewpoints but be an expert in conflict resolution!
- Create a sense of value (of each person) within the team where possible, giving each team member a specific responsibility however small the responsibility might seem.
- Enable the team members to be great at their job by providing them with the necessary tools and resources including job competence and ethical decision-making training. Help them develop their skills and become great team players too.
- Provide autonomy in the job but be available to help when requested. Provide continual individual and team appraisals,
- Encourage trust, goodwill, respect, and cooperation with and amongst the team members.
- Agree (by consensus, if possible) the ground rules with the team with regards to code of conduct, flexible working, timekeeping, work allocation etc. This will become the teams own "charter".
- A great leader will enable the members of her team to love their jobs and achieve great, impactful, and rewarding work.

A common theme in ALL aspects of culture is the importance of "the tone at the top" – which, while often referring to senior executive behaviour, can be applied to "those above me."

In a way senior leaders in a business have a "sacred trust." Not only do their decisions impact the shareholders – those whose money is invested in the company, they also affect many others internally and externally. Decision making by leaders has broad based implications. Everywhere – not just for investors. How a leader "sets the tone" impacts people's lives.

Step four: action the plan.

Some thought-provoking questions.
What are your thoughts and reflections on this chapter? Take some time to consider and possibly discuss with others.

The suggestion	Agree	Dis-agree	Let's Chat
One of our key challenges is implementation			
Some of the suggested "problems" (what goes wrong) apply to you?			
Some of the suggested actions will help embed the changes you want to implement.			
Are you developing an ongoing role for the Culture Change Committee?			
Has the board appointed someone with specific responsibility for culture?			
Is "discretionary compliance" understood and integrated as part of governance?			
Are the changes being sustained through training programs?			
Is "behaviour" a KEY aspect of all leadership development?			

Step four: action the plan.

Step four: action the plan.

8 Step five: continually improving.

8.1   Sustainability through continual improvement

This step emphasises the need for continual improvement We present the five-step approach as a "staircase" to emphasise that it requires a series of steps, each one building on the other.

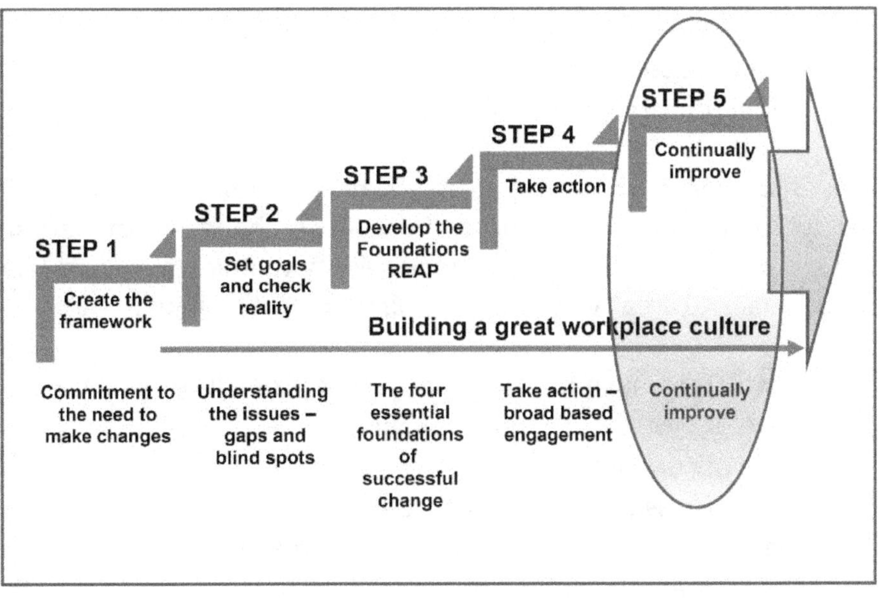

Step Five "takes us into the future" which may involve "circling back" and relooking at or possibly repeating earlier steps.

8.2   Never stop improving.

There is clearly no such thing as a perfect workplace culture. Nevertheless, it is important to have ambitious objectives and to always focus on continuous improvement by:

- Tracking progress against the strategic plan (for culture change) - update plan where necessary.
- Continue to assess via surveys and feedback, key issues such as:
    - Mental health, fair procedures, and policies.
    - Clarity and validity of the company vision and values.
    - The Code of Ethics – is it working and still relevant?
    - Whether everyone feels empowered to contribute their views.
    - Is adequate development and training taking place?
    - People taking personal responsibility for their actions.
    - Legal compliance.
- Communicate, communicate, communicate to all stakeholders.

Although companies may well develop their own pathway, the important thing to remember is that successful culture change must be part of a holistic and sustained strategy, supported by management and using the inspirational and creative energy of Champions for Change.

You should by now have fair and transparent procedures in place covering:
- Code of ethics and company values
- Code of conduct
- Ethical decision-making procedures
- Mental, physical, and financial health policies
- Recruitment and induction / orientation
- Fair pay and benefits structure
- Effective internal promotion structure
- Ethical supply chain procedure
- Strong bullying, harassment, and speak-up procedures.

Step five: continual improvement.

- Strong pro-environment procedures and strategy
- Effective and maintained training programme.
- Readily accessible and transparent EESG metrics
- Deeply embedded social purpose

You now have a Great Workplace Culture

The evolving workplace should reflect a place where "the way we do things around here" supports a positive and healthy workplace, and reflects:

- Employees who are proud of who they work for and will recommend the business to a friend.
- An organisation positioned to win the battle for talent - attract and retain top people with reduced costs of turnover and absenteeism.
- Improved mental and physical health and all the benefits that create:
    - Improved productivity – less absenteeism and presenteeism.
    - Employee performance (engagement, creativity, teamwork) is enhanced as they feel better about their workplace.
    - Improved levels of responsibility.
- An organisation trusted by suppliers, customers, and investors.
- A great reputation within the community and better customer loyalty.
- A more resilient ability in a crisis, leading to improved investor confidence – less likelihood of a scandal, litigation, being fined.
- Greater flexibility to respond to the need for change when required.
- Be ahead of the curve on legal compliance – laws are changing.
- Have a strong corporate purpose providing greater resilience in challenging times.
- Have a more sustainable and profitable business: responsible businesses in the medium term have better financial results and a more sustained profit.

Step five: continual improvement.

Planning and managing the culture is as strategically important as planning and managing both the business and social purpose. Culture, if not dealt with as a core part of strategy, will be allowed to evolve without direction, resulting in unpredictable and unplanned results and behaviours.

8.3   Embedding change in the business model

Closing the loop on continuous improvement requires integration of the framework for responsible business within the PDCA (Plan, Do, Check and Act) business model. "Checking" must include a clear linkage back to strategy and desired outcomes so that there is full visibility and accountability behind the desire to change and progress towards that goal. Chapter 11 discusses the holistic integration of Responsible Business "thinking" into an organizations business model.

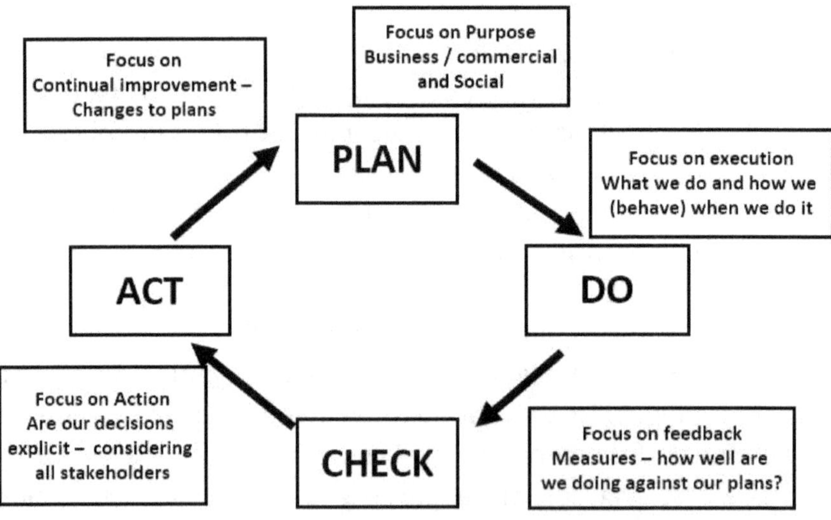

What is important in this integration is that there is equal focus on the business purpose – the commercial reasons that the organisation exists, and the social focus - in particular its behaviour as a member of society.

A key aspect of implementing an effective cultural change is developing a "check" approach that is fully aligned with the plans that have been established. If culture and behaviour isn't being checked regularly, then how can it be managed?

Critical to this is the development of a set of reporting metrics that cover BOTH progress against commercial plans – the processes, activities, tasks, and projects that people are engaged in doing to achieve the commercial purpose. PLUS progress against social purpose – the stated behaviours, driven by the code of ethics, responsible decision making and action by leadership that cover the organisations behaviour. Is the culture performing as planned?

The development of relevant metrics is covered in the Chapter 12 and can be used to help develop metrics that "populate" the "check" part of the business model. (Note that this discussion on metrics also covers the evolution of ESG reporting).

Do not "reinvent the wheel."
Many organisations already have continuous improvement of Kaizen as part of their quality management efforts. Where successful this will provide a solid basis for moving to "real Kaizen" – the culture and thinking that says everything is capable of improvement – but we must think that way.

Organisations may already have some system of metrics and performance reporting. This will form a solid basis – and the required metrics on behaviour and culture just needs to be added.

Some thought-provoking questions.

What are your thoughts and reflections on this chapter? Take some time to consider and possibly discuss with others.

The suggestion	Agree	Dis-agree	Let's Chat
Are there adequate safeguards to ensure continuous improvement?			
Do these safeguards apply to ALL aspects of the business model and the resources?			
Is continual improvement part of the PDCA Management model / framework?			
Are there approaches being taken to sustain enthusiasm for the culture shift?			
Are there regular discussions / communications with all stakeholders?			
Do you believe the right metrics are in place to evaluate and sustain "culture?"			

9 The case for responsible business

9.1   The case for responsible business

There are many serious challenges facing society and our world: climate change, poverty, inequality of opportunity and an inadequate education for millions to mention just a few. Climate change is clearly existential.

To help resolve these problems, the business sector must use its enormous influence and power, working alongside governments, investors, NGOs, and civil society. And do it quickly too.

In 2019, the US based Business Roundtable announced the release of a new <u>Statement on the Purpose of a Corporation</u> signed by 181 CEOs who commit to lead their companies for the benefit of all stakeholders – customers, employees, suppliers, communities and shareholders.

Since 1978, Business Roundtable has periodically issued Principles of Corporate Governance. Each version of the document issued since 1997 has endorsed principles of shareholder primacy – that corporations exist principally to serve shareholders. With today's announcement, the new Statement supersedes previous statements and outlines a modern standard for corporate responsibility.

It seems like the business sector, based on the above announcement knows that change is coming and that they need to respond. While the world has been talking about the social responsibility of business for almost half a century, business leaders are waking up to better define their PURPOSE. Not just to make money for investors but to make sure that the needs of

The case for Responsible Business.

ALL stakeholders are being considered. While this is a good step, there are many that cling to the view that business has NO responsibility other than to make money for its' shareholders. The renowned Milton Freidman has long been the focal point for these views.

> "There is one and only one social responsibility of business—to use its resources and engage in activities designed to increase its profits." That view has long influenced management thinking, corporate governance, and strategic moves.
>
> *Milton Friedman "The social responsibility of business..." September 13, 1970.*

But wait – further reading reveals that there is a "...but" in his writings that appear to suggest that while the rule of law is paramount, ethics remain important.

> In a free-enterprise, private-property system, a corporate executive is an employee of the owners of the business. He has direct responsibility to his employers. That responsibility is to conduct the business in accordance with their desires, which generally will be to make as much money as possible while conforming to their basic rules of the society, both those embodied in law and those embodied in ethical custom.

Two ESPECIALLY important phrases. *"Conduct the business in accordance with their (the owners) desires,"* and *"to make as much money as possible while conforming to their basic rules of the society, both those embodied in law and those embodied in ethical custom."*

So does business have BOTH a clear purpose, and is it operating within this framework, or has it drifted away?

The case for Responsible Business.

- Shareholders / investors are demanding greater transparency and accountability from business on both climate change and social issues.
- Governments are increasingly enacting laws and regulations to increase accountability from business on more than its financial performance.
- The UN has adopted a plan for achieving a better future for all — laying out a path over the next 15 years to end extreme poverty, fight inequality and injustice, and protect our planet.
- The UN further has global support for the changes needed and sees business as a driving force. It states: *"We are all in agreement on where the world needs to go. Fulfilling these ambitions will take an unprecedented effort by all sectors in society — and business must play a very important role in the process."*

Clearly the world is changing – but is business responding in an adequate way relative to its potential? Some might suggest either "no" or, as a minimum, progress is too slow. Some executives are taking action, but some seem to believe there are no problems and that their current solution is adequate.

- "Emissions Gap Report 2022: The Closing Window," finds that the international community is falling far short of the Paris climate goals, with no credible pathway to 1.5°C in place. Only an urgent system-wide transformation can avoid climate disaster. (Current performance will result in a 2.8% increase – almost double that needed)
- Violation Tracker UK contains more than 65,000 corporate files and penalties dating back to the beginning of 2010. Total monetary penalties in the last ten years, for businesses who broke the law, amount to £12.6 billion.
- The cost of fines and penalties imposed In the USA from their current list of the top ten most penalized (fines and penalties) companies shows 1,712 cases and a cost of $301 BILLION.

- Despite pressing concerns from consumers, 52 per cent of UK businesses don't currently have a clear CSR (Corporate Social Responsibility) strategy set out. (Fintech Times, 2022).
- Exxon was aware of climate change, as early as 1977, 11 years before it became a public issue. …this knowledge did not prevent the company (now ExxonMobil and the world's largest oil and gas company) from spending decades refusing to publicly acknowledge climate change and even promoting climate misinformation (Scientific American).
- The International Monetary Fund estimates that avoidance of corporation tax (using tax havens and "gaming" differences in international tax rules and regulations, (sic),), is costing national governments between $500 and $600 billion annually.

Are these demonstrations of responsible business activity? If not, they must be irresponsible. Hence the need for a renewed effort to enhance Responsible Business. To move faster. To look for better ways. To seek and eliminate the root causes of why progress is not fast enough. Nor is it creating a fairer and more just society.

9.2   We NEED business.

Our quest is not anti-business, in fact the opposite. We are concerned that the positive and successful aspects of business will be lost if conduct and social accountability are not re-invigorated. Business is a "big thing."

According to government statistics there were 5.5 million private sector businesses in the UK at the start of 2022. Most of these businesses are small, with less than 50 employees (5.47million), 35,900 are medium sized enterprises and 7,700 are large organisations. Small businesses employ 48% of the population, while large organisations employ 39%.

Turnover / Sales are about £4.1 Trillion; direct employment is about 27 million. In 2021/22 UK Corporation tax paid by business was £68 billion (with business rates – taxes based on non-residential property) amounted to over £22 billion.

In 2021 UK exports totalled £654 billion, supporting an overall economy (GDP) of £2.2 trillion.

If one were to look at other major economies a similar picture would emerge of business being a major economic driving force of value and wealth creation. Business is needed as a core factor in the economic system – but its performance and behaviour need to be consistently evaluated and assessed and adjusted to reflect its place in society.

9.3   Business behaviour could be better.

We contend that as Global Citizens, the business sector must accept its responsibilities towards people and planet issues as well as making an ethical profit. So, many companies will need to change their focus, currently primarily on profit, by taking more responsibility for these other issues. People and planet issues are a responsibility, not a choice.

This objective, to aspire to be a responsible business, must become the primary purpose of an organisation. It is self-evident that more working people making responsible decisions day-in, day-out will make the world a better place to live and work. No-one can do everything but, for sure, everyone can do something.

We know there are increasingly large numbers of passionate and visionary people who support this objective (to be a responsible business) too.

We argue that is only with the foundation of a great workplace culture that businesses be able to make the changes the world so desperately and urgently needs. The purpose of this book is to offer a workable, practical solution to creating a great workplace culture.

9.4   UN Social Development Goals

A series of Sustainable Development Goals (SDGs) were adopted in 2015 by the 193 United Nations (UN) member states. That is 100% adoption. Global commitment. There are seventeen goals which address economic, environmental, and social impacts, and are designed to form a blueprint for good growth, nationally and internationally, by 2030. These goals have already been referenced by many organizations that declare they have a social purpose, and that purpose aligns with and supports the UN goals. (This is why our goal is Responsible Business 2030.

In their statement ***All Companies Can Play a Role,*** the UN states the following:

No matter how large or small, and regardless of their industry, all companies can contribute to the SDGs. While the scale and scope of the global goals is unprecedented, the fundamental ways that business can contribute remain unchanged. The UN Global Compact asks companies to first do business responsibly and then pursue opportunities to solve societal challenges through business innovation and collaboration.

Global challenges – ranging from climate, water, and food crises, to poverty, conflict, and inequality – are in need of solutions that the private sector can deliver, representing a large and growing market for business innovation. In the rush to transform business models and systems for the future, integrity and values will have a huge role to play. For companies wanting to advance the SDG agenda, the job starts by acting responsibly – incorporating the Ten Principles of the UN Global Compact widely into strategies and operations and understanding that good practices or innovation in one area cannot make up for doing harm in another.

The UN states that *"the new Global Goals result from a process that has been more inclusive than ever, with Governments involving business, civil society, and citizens from the outset. We are all in agreement on where the world needs to go. Fulfilling these ambitions will take an unprecedented effort by all sectors in society — and business must play a very important role in the process."*

By looking through each of the SDG's, some level of linkage can be determined that should tie into the strategic plan of a business. Here are some examples based on the SDG's.

Social Development Goals 1 to 6
Let's look at the first six SDG's.

Are there any of the first six goals above that an organization could align with its' business purpose? Good health and well – being, goal # 3 – how about health and safety in the workplace including mental health?

How about goal #4 quality education? In a fast-changing world of "lifelong learning" what role does business play? We have already determined that a great workplace culture is one that encourages personal development and growth.

How about number 6, gender equality. While many governments have brought in legislation and many organisations report on compliance to gender equality expectations, what does it look like INSIDE the business? Let us focus less on compliance and more on the culture and climate in the workplace – ensuring equal opportunity and no discrimination. Do people treat each other with equality? Do managers and supervisors actually behave with equality in their attitudes, comments, actions, and decision making?

Social Development Goals 7 through 12
How about the next six?

Certainly, for many organisations, decent work (number 8) would be applicable? This would be creating a "great workplace – safety and no harm both physically and mentally.

Goal #10 is a fitting example where many organizations claim to abide by inclusion and diversity, yet people are treated poorly and discriminated against internally. Why? There may be policies and procedures in place to ensure equality in hiring and promotion – yet unless individuals within the business treat each other with fairness and equity, then the UN goal and societal expectations are not being achieved.

Goal 12 Responsible Consumption and production is clearly an area where business has a role. Not to produce products that clearly cause irresponsible behaviour such as plastic bags and non-recyclable products. Irresponsible consumption is at the heart of business role in climate change. The whole concept of externalities is to move away from the traditional approach of not worrying about consumption (or emissions) if there was no direct financial implication – in other words if the shareholder was not being directly impacted.

Social Development Goals 13 through17
How about the last five goals?

Goal 16, Peace, Justice, and Strong Institutions; this goal might lead to a long debate about the role of business in sustaining democracy. Once again "respect for the law" as well as the various institutions including regulatory activity might be part of a responsible business. Also, to have strong institutions we need strong, professional and ethical approaches to governance.

Clearly the world is undergoing a broad-based change. Some might argue that all the above being social goals are not the responsibility of business. However, as the day-to-day operations of a business impact the lives of both those directly impacted such as investors, employees, suppliers, customers, and others, they also impact those external to the business.

This role of business in society has become even more complex as business is now "ultra-national" operating in multiple societies often with different expectations, laws, and cultures.

A Responsible Business recognizes these changes and modifies its governance framework and operations accordingly.

10 Guidance: creating a Code of Ethics

Creating a Code of Ethics is an essential part of the work of the Culture Change Committee, which has identified the existing culture and started to develop an understanding of the "desired culture" (the "future state") in determining the gap analysis. This part of the action plan will be to close the gap between reality and the desired state is a statement that clarifies expectations.

Understanding the organisations shared values is an important first step in developing a Code. There must be agreement in what is important to most people in the organisation before a code has any potential for success. Once a set of values has been developed, shared, and mutually agreed, a code of ethics which reflects and embodies many of the values can be created. Before we start, let's have a brief clarification on definitions:

- Personal or life values are the foundation of an *individual person's* ability to judge between right and wrong. Values are based on a deep-rooted system of beliefs that guide a person's decisions. Values form an individual foundation that influences a particular person's behaviour. Examples include integrity, friendship, commitment.
- Moral values emerge out of core values. *Morals are specific and context-driven rules that govern a person's desire to be good*. They can be shared by a larger population, but a person's moral code may

differ from others' depending on their personal values. Examples are "its bad to steal" and "it's good to help a friend in need."

- Ethics guide and determine what behaviours are "right" or "wrong." While many believe that morals and ethics are similar, ethics dictate what practical behaviours are allowed, but our "moral code" reflect our intentions. Examples include the medical profession's "do no harm" and an accountant's commitment to client confidentiality.

You are thinking "this gets quite complicated!" It does take some learning and it is a complex subject – but it is very important to do the research and have the discussions.

Framework for defining values.
Values are a key factor in driving individual behaviour and decision making. When we make personal decision, these will usually take into account our own personal values and beliefs, (unless we act implicitly, by rote and don't think about it).

Similarly, organisational values are a common set of shared beliefs that reflect an organisation's identity and personality and shape its behaviours. They define the expectations against which actual behaviour will be judged.

As individuals, we acquire personal values throughout our lives. They can also change over time. They answer the question "what do you believe in?" These beliefs will impact how we make decisions. While individuals may

Trusting	Supportive	Positive
Open	Cooperative	Collaborative
Fun	Fair	Honest
Sharing	Challenging	Equality
Ethical	Caring	Authentic
Competent	Inclusive	Safe
Diverse	Accountable	Considerate
Responsible		Respectful

have different values, in general many values are shared within each society. Here are some examples:

Ethics are similar but are "unwritten rules" about what is morally and socially acceptable within a society. People growing up in a particular society or even a certain family will tend to have their personal values impacted by what their family or society accepts as morally right.

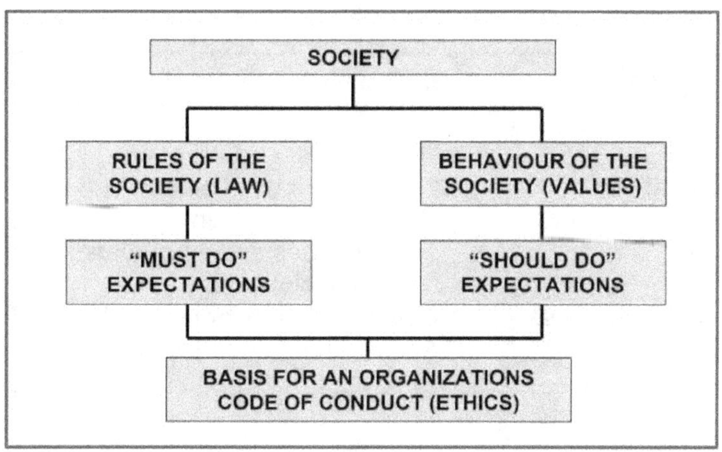

Why are corporate moral and ethical values so important? These values form the "human" heart and soul of an organisation. Organisations are composed of a collection of people who have come together for a common and shared purpose. Values are the core principles that set the tone and shape its culture and activities.

Values also express how an organisation will interact with clients, partners, and employees, and form the basis of decision making on how it chooses to achieve its objectives. Shared values are a significant aspect of building trust within a group. Trust leads to higher levels of cooperation, collaboration, and engagement that ultimately leads to a higher level of predictability in behaviour ad higher productivity.

Defining values should be a co-creation of leadership and the workforce base, ideally done in an engaging and interactive way. Thus, the Culture Change Committee can be a leading champion and catalyst in this work.

Here are two lasting statements of values from Kellogg's and IKEA. Others have embedded their values into a much longer statement. An example is Johnson & Johnson – known as J&J. They have a "credo" which was created 1943 and which still forms their foundational values.

Kellogg's	IKEA
Integrity Accountability Passion Humility Simplicity A focus on success	Humbleness and willpower. Leadership by example. Daring to be different. Togetherness and enthusiasm. Cost-consciousness. Constant desire for renewal. Accept and delegate responsibility.

The exercise to develop and agree upon a set of values cannot be taken lightly. It will take time and effort. Once they are publicised, the organisation has made it known that those values are what it stands for. So they need to be accurate and suit the ambitions of your "unique" business.

Typically, organisational values will likely last for years to come, although as society changes, certain values may shift. This should require a periodic review to make sure the values being used as a foundation for behaviour do in fact still reflect societal expectations.

Creating a set of moral values has several purposes. First, it helps to define an understanding of what is "acceptable" in the business in terms of attitudes, behaviours and decision making. It is a basis for "the way we do things around here." It also provides guidance when hiring people into the organisation. Clearly people who do not share the values will have a challenge in working with others and building trust.

Creating the Code of Ethics

A Code of Ethics (CoE) consists of a set of principles designed to guide employees in what is right and wrong and to assist in their decision-making. The creation of a CoE is an integral part of creating a great workplace culture and complements and supports the chosen values that have been agreed.

- The Code should be created by the Culture Change Committee or by an Ethics Committee.
- The Code must be based on consultation with employees, and address the results of the staff survey, focus groups, discussion and agreement with management and the Board and agreement on the Values.
- The CoE will be unique to each organisation and will essentially define the culture of the organisation – "how we do things around here".
- The final CoE must be approved, endorsed, and acted upon by the Board of Directors.
- The CoE should be short and general in nature.
- The CoE must be promoted to all staff and other stakeholders on a regular basis. **The CoE must be in the DNA of the business.**
- The CoE should be reassessed (but not necessarily changed) on a regular basis – certainly every two years.
- The CoE could be supported by a more detailed Code of Conduct which determines rules, regulations and responsibilities and directs and guides the employees in various matters.

The discussions that take place around this subject will be challenging. People with have differing opinions. The people who are part of the organisation may disagree on certain issues. In most cases there is no "right or wrong" – it is an opinion and it needs to be debated and consensus arrived at.

Signing the pledge to adhere to a Code of Ethics

After consultation and approval with your employees, it is recommended that employees are requested to sign a PLEDGE agreeing to abide by the Code of Ethics.

This can either be achieved by employees being required to sign an actual copy of the stated code with their commitment to abide by it, or as a certification that they have read the code, understand its implications and responsibilities, and agree to abide by it as a condition of employment.

The challenge is that while many organisations have codes in place, and even have employees sign them, they fail to become an integral and valued part of the governance framework of the organisation. They don't become "the way we do business" in reality.

ENRON in the USA was an example of this problem. The company had a Code of Ethics, of over sixty pages that employees all signed – including the CEO but which was clearly not part of reality.

In the UK the collapse of Carillion several years ago, clearly illustrates the importance of having a code.

The Collapse of Carillion - a Failure of Ethical Standards?

As further details emerge about the collapse of Carillion, it is tempting to put their failures down to a lack of poor strategic leadership and competent financial management. Details supporting that thesis may well emerge over the coming months as various bodies and Select Committees carry out their investigations. But that focus, important though it is, should not detract from an examination of what an absence of ethical leadership, honesty, transparency and accountability has cost the company, government and taxpayer and above all, its employees, subcontractors and those who rely on the public services it was contracted to provide.

An example of an agreement to abide by a code by National Grid.

National Grid:

I have read and understand National Grid's 'Doing the Right Thing, our Standards of Ethical Business Conduct'. I am complying with the Standards now and intend to continue to comply with them in the future. The information on this form is complete and accurate, but if circumstances should change, I will inform the Business Conduct and Ethics Office promptly in writing.

Since the collapse of Carillion, the call for effective Codes of Conduct or Ethics has increased as being an essential aspect of corporate governance.

Example of a Code

There is no substitute for the process of developing a unique code of ethics for each organisation. This example that follows is purely illustrative of the type of wording that might be used.

In this example three sections have been used to align with the pillars of a Responsible Business.

People

- I will play my part, within my sphere of influence, in the company commitment to ensure all staff enjoy their work, are motivated, well-trained, physically and psychologically safe, have equal opportunities, a great life balance and are fairly paid.

- I will behave responsibly towards my colleagues, the company, customers, suppliers and the wider society with care, respect, integrity and compassion at all times.

- I will not undertake nor ask a colleague to undertake any illegal or unethical behaviour.

- I will work with my colleagues and other key stakeholders to develop and improve the company's social purpose and to meet the company's social purpose targets.

While the wording expresses "I" versus "we" or "our organization," ___each would be valid if the individuals sign the document___. The individual signing the document is making a personal commitment – taking personal responsibility.

Additionally, this statement assumes that people know what the code of ethics contains as it is clearly in another document – or maybe it was used in the orientation training and all employees signed it at that point.

The next section deals with the planet aspects – environment, culture change – whatever "label" each organisation wants to place on it.

Planet

- I will consider the ethical implications, as well as legal, in all my decisions and work practices, which have an environmental impact.
- I will play my part in the company commitment to meet the Company's published environmental targets.
- I will work with colleagues and other key stakeholders to develop and improve the company's contribution to the environment.
- I will play my part in ensuring the introduction of environmental management, measurement and reporting systems that provides the structures and processes that embed environmental efficiently into the company's culture.

Once again here there is an assumption that employees are made aware of the environmental targets – but the key statement is that each person is taking personal responsibility for decisions that impact the environment positively.

Profit

- I will play my part, within my sphere of influence, in meeting commercial targets via an ethical, socially responsible and environmentally sustainable business strategy.
- I will play my part in ensuring that sustainability issues are embedded into the governance and decision-making process of the company.

Guidance on creating a Code of Ethics.

This clarifies the personal commitment to adopting approaches and attitudes that support the ethical principles as well as the commercial business plan.

Business benefits of having a Code of Ethics

As codes become more commonplace, the connection between effective governance, in particular risk management is being realized. The larger the organisation the more important having a defined and documented code.

- Clarification of and foundation for behavioural expectations
- Base for consistency in hiring, leadership, and performance evaluation
- Personal pride that leaders/employees do not hurt people or the environment to achieve their objectives. **Do Good – Do No Harm**.
- Battle for talent - attract and retain top people.
- Improved mental and physical health and all the benefits that creates.
  - Improved productivity – less absenteeism and presenteeism.
  - Employee performance (engagement, creativity, teamwork) is enhanced as they feel better about their workplace.
  - Improved levels of responsibility.
- Improved supplier/partner trust.
- Positive reputation within the community and better customer loyalty.
- Improved investor confidence – less likelihood of a scandal, litigation, being fined.
- Ethical businesses in the medium term have better financial results.

Once stated and documented, the code will create expectations of behaviour against which the organization can be assessed. However, part of the value in being willing to use this as a base, is the ability to assess actual performance such as leadership's ability to build positive relationships.

Decision making should now become more explicit – based on consideration of the mutually agreed and stated Code of Ethics. Rather than using generic questions in employee surveys about the foundation for behaviour and decision making, questions can be specifically created that validate against the stated code.

How a Code of Ethics impacts decision making.

ALL decision making is impacted by a combination of personal / shared values and the organisations mutually agreed code. All decisions whether at an interpersonal level or as part of the boardroom strategy should be based on the company's Code of Ethics. We need to consider:

- Personal decisions.
- Decisions related to how we interact with others in the workplace.
- Commercial and business decisions and
- Corporate strategic and operational decisions.

<table>
<tr>
<td>

PERSONAL
Decision making

- Behaving with goodwill towards others
- Being respectful
- Compassionate
- Responsible decision-making

</td>
<td>

WORKPLACE CULTURE
Behaviour of the group

- Inclusion and diversity – race, gender, age, physical ability, etc.
- Fairness
- Social purpose
- Levels of moral awareness
- Ethical leadership – lead from the top
- Ethical sourcing

</td>
</tr>
<tr>
<td>

COMMERCIAL
Business decisions

- Paying suppliers on time
- Real living wage and fair pay
- Employee well-being
- Paying a fair rate of tax
- No zero hours contracts
- Treating customers and suppliers fairly at all times

</td>
<td>

CORPORATE DECISIONS
On major societal issues

- Sustainable Development Goals
- Human rights issues such as child labour and modern slavery
- Environmental issues and climate change

</td>
</tr>
</table>

Applying ethical standards to decision making in business becomes more important as competitive pressures start to encourage compliance only with legal requirements and encourage ignoring ethical issues. After all, the legal system and court decisions can only take action when compliance with the law is in question.

A Responsible Business is one where the challenge of acting ethically rather than only focusing on legality, is taken seriously – is part of the DNA.

It is extremely hard to act ethically when your competitors may be gaining competitive advantage by taking action that is clearly unethical but is unseen by society in general. Employees who know about it would see that it was "not right" because it goes against what people believe in as a foundation for behaviour in a civilized society. Examples below above illustrate the problem:

- Organizations are late (contractually) paying suppliers because it has become normal practise.
- Supply chains include unethical or irresponsible suppliers because there are no ethical requirements required as a condition of supply.
- Senior managers are seen to ignore policies or procedures because they can "get away with it."
- Corporate governance (boards) focus on financial performance and related risks and ignore other aspects of the business stakeholders.
- Supervisors take credit for suggestions made by employees to gain personal career benefits.
- Supervisors discriminate against certain people that they "don't like" for some reason.
- Individuals fail to own up to problems or blame others.

There is no end of examples of where reality fails to meet ethical expectations. The "Good Business Charter" accreditation organisation spells out ten principles that form the basis for their foundations' approach. These are:

- Real living wage
- Fairer hours and contracts
- Employee well-being
- Employee representation
- Diversity and inclusion
- Environmental responsibility
- Pay fair tax.
- Commitment to customers
- Ethical sourcing
- Prompt payment to suppliers.

Establishing these underlying commitments to "behaving responsibly" are critical. This is where management / leadership becomes important. Both for leading by example as well as taking action in cases of non-conformance. Taking action is often not seeking to discipline someone, but taking the time and effort to understand why an employee made a certain decision and using the situation or event as a learning experience. (Continual improvement).

One major challenge is in ensuring that the words and phrases used in a Code of Ethics as well as stated Values are understood and interpreted by people in a similar manner. It takes time to build the expectations into the operational DNA and one key, practical aspect that Responsible Organizations should use is an operational reality check.

Often referred to as an "is / is not" statement, this approach converts the stated principles into representative actions. The following example may help to demonstrate how an organisation can discuss and "operationalise" its code and what the words mean in practice.

^{An} **EduVision Inc.** _{Knowledge Service}	Sample	Organizational Values Development Discussion
Values statements version dated		

6. To be recognized as a leader in our relationships with employees	
Means (Is)	**Is not**
❑ To provide equal opportunity for advancement ❑ To have an open door policy ❑ To respond to concerns in a timely manner ❑ To demonstrate care, respect and acknowledgement for all employees ❑ To provide a safe workplace from every perspective - physically, emotionally & mentally ❑ To set clear guidelines for expected performance and behaviour ❑ To be consistent in our approach to discipline and rewarding performance ❑ To ensure continued support of company social club activities ❑ To maintain a high level of employee satisfaction and low turnover ❑ Fostering trust, communication and inclusiveness	❑ Allowing employees to circumvent Company policies, procedures and rules ❑ Inconsistency in dealing with employees at different plants ❑ Accepting the minimum required performance of employees ❑ Deviating from our Values in dealing with employees nor allowing employees to engage in activities "disrespectful" of our Values

In this example, the value being discussed by the organisation was number six on their list which stated they wanted "To be recognized as leader in our relationship with employees." The value sounded simple.

It soon became apparent that not everybody interpreted the statement the same way. A discussion with both employees and management focused on asking "what would we be doing if we actually demonstrated this value on a day-to-day basis?" Likewise, "what sort of decision making, and actions would detract from people believing in the value statement?" Results provided several examples that would be seen as positive or negative in decisions and action.

This type of discussion about what the "stated words" actually mean in terms of day-to-day behaviour form an important part of engaging people in the process. They can start to recognise how their own daily work is impacted by a Code of Ethics. This start to avoid the problem that is so widespread where organisations have Codes of Ethics – often prominently displayed, yet employees will say "that is not what we actually do." This need to be conducted from the Board level down through the organisation.

A Responsible Business does not make assumptions that people know what you mean but creates an open forum where clarification can be continually discussed.

11 Guidance: business model

Some readers may be concerned that the five-step approach that has been described in some way adds a burden to the existing way a business is run.

This is wrong. If applied effectively the five-step approach becomes fully integrated INTO the business model. It BECOMES the way we do things around here. The change in culture becomes an integral part of every step of managing the business. How plans are made. How action and execution is conducted. How performance and progress is measured, and how day-to-day decision making takes place.

In several sections we talked about being effective and stated that the steps taken must be holistic. This chapter describes how that can be achieved by embedding the thinking of the five-step process into a traditional business model.

This starts at the planning stage where the organisation plans not just its' business purpose but its broad-based purpose in terms of society. It thinks not just about business purpose in terms of the products and services to be produced but more broadly on the way that the organisation will behave and the way that their actions will impact all stakeholders and not just shareholders.

11.1   The Five steps and the PDCA business model

The five-step approach this book suggests, is a strategic culture change approach, focused on building a better business culture that will lead to a more responsible business. It must therefore be built in as a core aspect of business strategy and to do that it must be seen in the context of an overall business model. The best known and simplest is the PDCA or Plan, Do, Check and Act model.

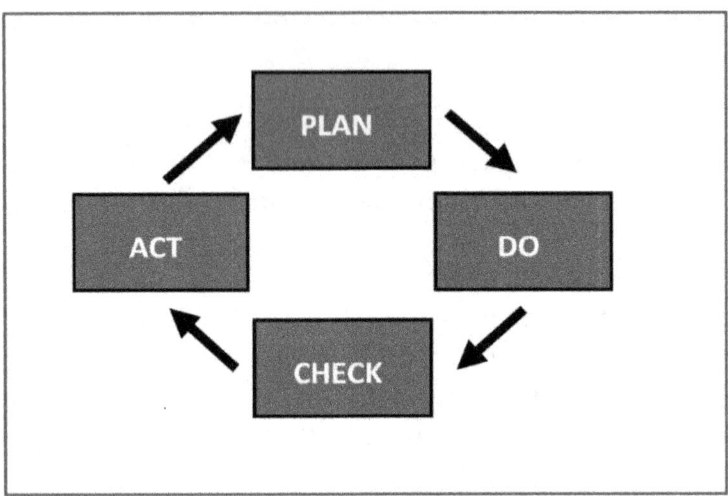

Plan

Everything starts with planning. Where are we now? What is the reality that surrounds us? What is the need for change and what changes do we need to make? How are we going to make the required changes? In terms of our culture change initiative, many of the tasks from the five-step process will be part of the planning stage. That will lead the organisation to the "Do" or action phase.

Do

The "Do" segment is critically important. This is where the desired approaches to day-to-day operational decision-making take place. This is where the desired actions will become reality. This is where employee involvement and engagement happen. Typically, this is the point where a substantial proportion of change initiatives fail. Intent is not turned into reality.

This is the place where one-on-one interaction between people takes place. It is these "moments of truth", and the behaviour individuals exhibit that determines whether a commitment to becoming a responsible business happen or are ignored.

This is also the part of the business model where policies, processes, and procedures are implemented. If these are not aligned with the commitment to being a responsible business, then once again reality will not reflect the desired intent. Have all the organisations policies, processes, and procedures been checked and aligned with the desired "way we (want to) do things around here" to support the achievement of becoming a responsible business?

Have leaders at every single level bought into and committed to delivering a consistent message? Having the right people in leadership roles who demonstrate the stated commitments to being a responsible business, and who demonstrate these in their inter-action with others and their decision making are probably THE MOST CRITICAL ASPECT of achieving the goal of being a responsible business.

Check
The "check" aspect of the business model is where the measurement, assessment and validation take place. These "checks" provide management with information that assures them that their plans are being executed successfully or that certain areas need to be addressed because results are not as desired. Progress against goals and objectives is monitored.

What to measure and how to measure are hot topics for business today. As has been discussed in Chapters 9 and 12, new requirements for measurement and reporting in areas like ESG are being mandated. Does the organisation have the right measures and indicators to assess whether their commitment to being a responsible business is being delivered?

Act

Finally, the "act" stage reflects the continual improvement that takes place but in terms of day-to-day corrective action to ensure plans stay on track as well as the more strategic learning that takes place and feeds back into the planning stage of the business model at the next iteration.

11.2 Combining business and social purpose

There is no need to change the business model. PDCA works just fine. What is needed is to make sure that the content includes BOTH a focus on achievement of the core *business purpose* (to make a healthy ethical profit) *PLUS achievement of the behaviour*, culture and operational methodology that drives a responsible business. This means that at every step the duality of purpose must be addressed.

		BUSINESS PURPOSE	SOCIAL PURPOSE
P	PLAN	TASK. Purpose, goals and objectives	BEHAVIOUR. Goals and objectives
D	DO	People, processes and core resources	Leadership and relationships
C	CHECK	Operational metrics	Behavioural metrics
A	ACT	Process, activity, resource actions	Human behavioural action / development

This illustration above shows a version of PDCA that reflects the duality of strategy and the thinking that underpins becoming a responsible business.

Note that at each stage of PDCA, PURPOSE remains the driver – but as a driver of both WHAT we do (our business purpose) and HOW WE DO IT (our social purpose – acting as a responsible member of society). This is all about how we make decisions. How the organisation is seen to behave. How it goes about performing its day-to-day activities. How it builds relationships with its' partners – both on the supply side (vendors in the supply chain) and demand side – its customers.

This duality is embedded at every stage of the business management model. If becoming responsible is not embedded in strategy and every aspect of the business model, it will fail. This is evidenced by the significant "lapses" in behaviour that occur, even though the plans might have been in place. Plans like having a Code of Ethics which are part of the foundations – but where there is no link between what the code says the organisation is committed to and the decisions that are made by leaders on a daily basis. Intent fails to become reality.

The overall governance framework of the business must reflect the commitment to act responsibly. This requires both compliance to legal requirements as well as recognition of, and compliance with other requirements that drive behaviour and decision making.

Planning

Referring to the business model, those in leadership positions – board and executive, must ensure that at the planning stage, equal attention is given to the task and the behaviour. "What we do and how we will behave doing it."

Planning is at the core of "intent." A plan sets out what an organisation wants to do. Traditionally plans have focused on achievement of the **business** purpose. This involves setting business goals and objectives and then designing a business model that is "fit for purpose" When plans are silent on social purpose, there is no guidance on what sort of tactics especially behaviours are "allowed" or expected to achieve the goals. If guidance is needed on what we do, it is even more needed on how we do it. How we behave and function as a responsible citizen.

P	**PLAN**	**TASK. Purpose, goals and objectives**	**BEHAVIOUR. Goals and objectives**

When a business plan is prepared it should take into account all stakeholders. This includes the impact on society that results from the way in which the business operates. It includes products, services, markets, customers, operations. Everything.

A responsible business plan would be one that is broad based and sets goals and objectives for both what is- to be achieved – the business outcomes, as well as how it will be achieved in terms of other outcomes. Most obvious would be "no harm" – to people, suppliers, communities, climate, and others.

By staying silent on non-financial or other stakeholders' aspects, assumptions about what is acceptable will be made. This will result in surprises. People will act unethically. Staff will get harassed. Suppliers will be abused. Products will continue to be produced that have a negative impact on society.

<u>Doing</u> – putting the plan into action

Once plans are in place, management converts these into operational tactics – the strategies, plans and actions needed to deliver the desired goals and objectives. Traditionally this involves deciding on projects, processes, activities, and tasks that need to be performed to deliver results. Resources need to be obtained as inputs to the work to be done – including a workforce.

Compliance with legal requirements is typically a criterion defined within which management must operate. Examples are complying with health and safety standards and labour laws around employment. While there may be a Code of Ethics – if it has not been "operationalised" by being fully integrated into policies and procedures it might well be irrelevant to people in their day-to-day actions and decisions. Examples of where "failure to integrate" can cause problems include:

- Hiring policies are in place about diversity, but managers promote, and reward staff based on personal bias.
- Policies are in place about fairness and inclusion but managers provide opportunities, promotions and overtime to a select few.
- Policies are in place related to harassment, but female employees continue to be subjected to harassment, suggestions, and innuendo.
- A commitment is made to work / life balance but work schedules caused by understaffing to save money, create unreasonable workloads.
- A customer pays a bill twice, and staff are told to keep quiet unless they notice and ask for a refund.
- Even though suppliers have contracts with thirty day terms, they are paid up to three months late.
- The company underbids contracts to get the work, knowing that once work has started the customer will have minimal leverage to avoid cost escalations.
- Capital equipment is purchased, made principally on cost and financial benefit, but minimising aspects of environmental considerations.

D	DO	People, processes and core resources	Leadership and relationships

A critical aspect of effectively integrating business purpose and social purpose is to create conditions around behaviours that relate to inter-personal relations. How people are treated on a day-to-day basis.

Critical within the "do" or operational execution stage, is leadership. Effective leaders, trained to follow a code of ethics and make responsible decisions. A senior management that affirms and supports the commitment to follow the defined plans. Both are at the leading edge of "making it real."

Leaders that focus on both management of processes and supporting resources with an equal focus to how people are being treated and engaged. Every interaction that takes place is a "moment of truth."

Relationships must be built to set a climate for responsible as well as flawless execution. A responsible business focuses on managing both tangibles (outputs and outcomes of products and services) and intangibles (outcomes in terms of quality and strength of relationships as well as growth and well-being of people involved).

A responsible business will ensure that its focus on business outcomes carry equal importance and weight to all other outcomes.

Check. **Are we "on plan?"**
The third stage of the business model deals with checking – usually done by the types of metrics used to monitor performance. These aspects are discussed in Chapter 12 that provide some suggested approaches to metrics.

However, metrics are not the only source of obtaining feedback on "how we are doing" against the plans. Talking to employees and obtaining their input is critical to discovering underlying issues. (This is one reason why world class companies such as Toyota place such a high priority on the supervisor – employee relationship).

The "C" aspect – checking, must be holistic covering both operational performance as well as workplace climate and consistency of behaviours. Measures like "taking the pulse" of the level of workforce commitment, assessing individual levels of engagement and encouraging people to speak up and speak out when problems arise are so critical. It's about monitoring both the performance AND the culture.

A responsible business will ensure that feedback systems are in place to check on all aspects of organisational goals, objectives, and outcomes. This will include:

- Traditional quantitative feedback on outputs and outcomes (time, quality, cost, and quantity).
- Financial performance against plans.
- Levels of employee engagement, turnover, and others.
- Health and tenure of the workforce.
- Environmental aspects and impacts
- Leadership effectiveness – including reinforcement of desired behaviour according to values and code of ethics.
- Supplier relationships
- Customer relationships
- Brand and reputation

A broad-based approach will ensure that management and the board remain aware of organisational performance both in terms of the business purpose as well as the reality and perceptions of behaviour as observed by other stakeholders.

<u>Act</u> – Decision making and action.
Finally, the "A" part of the business model. Action. How does management respond to problems and issues. Behaviour once again is a key ingredient.

Earlier the issues of explicit or implicit actions were discussed. How people act will either be "thought" and fact driven or reactive. So often in business de-motivation, loss of morale and reluctance to "go the extra mile" can come from leaders' behaviour when decisions are made.

Leaders are human beings as are all employees. Being so, we are all prone to being reactive – making decisions without thinking it through. Worse still, the reality is that decisions are often made in times of pressure and stress, and people can act emotionally rather than logically when this occurs.

Peoples' unique personalities also play a part. It is a proven fact that human behaviour can change under stress – and a leader may behave consistently with the values and ethics code 95% of the time – but there will be times when they react badly.

If a leader has built a positive, trusting relationship with staff, and allows dialogue and feedback, people will tend to allow for these occasional situations. But if a leader also believes they are "never wrong" and cannot admit mistakes, that creates a problem. These situations – the 5% where the leader either "loses it" or makes a mistake, can be learning experiences if they cause the leader to ask, "how could I have managed that better?"

A — ACT	Process, activity, resource actions	Human behavioural action / development

So, when we act and make decisions, we either reinforce the code of ethics and the values or we run the risk of demonstrating to people that these are "not rules for me but for everybody else." In acting to resolve both process, activity and resource issues, or organisational behaviour issues, responsible decision-making focuses on facts and root causes. Then moves to resolve the issue.

A leader can develop a personal checklist to think through how they respond to situations they are faced with when making decisions:

- Does "action" reinforce the organisational values and code of ethics?
- Do inter-actions include clear communication, and supportive collaboration?
- If people are missing targets, are they berated and disciplined or coached and supported? (Are we in the "blame game?")
- If the company is missing targets, is it "cost cutting focused" rather than searching for underlying root causes?
- If reputation or brand feedback is declining, is it a PR / greenwashing approach or a soul searching about underlying culture and the quality of relationships?
- Do decisions consider all key stakeholders?
- Would the results of decision made, and action taken be seen as responsible?

Unethical behaviour

There are many scandals reported about organisations behaving unethically – the question is "what was the motivation?" One key to a responsible business is managing risk – the less action taken to prevent unethical behaviour the greater the probability of it happening. This is at the heart of implementing the foundations (REAP) to a responsible business.

- **Worst case** – no guidance, no hiring criteria, no leadership guidance. Unethical behaviour seen by leaders as "part of the game of business." Unethical behaviour likely to occur.
- **Substantial risk** – Code of Ethics created but no linkage to hiring or supervisory training; internal climate of "do what management tells you, and don't question it."

- **Elevated Risk** – Code of Ethics in place and signed by staff – but no reinforcement through management nor any assessment feedback.
- **Some Risk** – Code of Ethics in place. Testing at time of hiring. Embedded in supervisory training, leadership assessments and compensation. (But) ethical questions are elevated to management who make decisions based on business imperative notwithstanding potential code violations.
- **Lowest risk** – as above and management actively and publicly make decisions clearly linked to stated Code of Ethics.

Organisations may want to rank themselves against some of these factors to see what their "behavioural risk profile" looks like. Considering the above, unethical issues or even illegal activities may still happen because:

- It was an honest mistake or misunderstanding.
- There has been a lapse in reinforcement or training.
- The organisation leadership has changed, and new leaders do not believe in the Code of Ethics as a guide to behaviour.
- Someone has personal problems or issues that led them to act this way.

There may be others – but you get the point. Having the Code of Ethics embedded in the DNA will lessen the risk – but you can never totally eliminate it. A responsible business will do everything it can to avoid having ethical problems.

12 Guidance: metrics.

Stakeholders are demanding greater transparency and reporting from business supported by more and more metrics related to environment, social and governance aspects. This data has to be tracked, extracted, analysed, and reported and this is becoming very expensive and time consuming. The key goal is to use the KISS (Keep It Short and Simple) approach.

Various groups of people (investors, employees, consumers, government, environmentalists) are looking, with a variety of different objectives, for companies with values that demonstrate a responsible and sustainable strategy towards human rights issues and environmental due diligence.

In order to avoid the costly provision of metrics that are of no interest to anyone, the following list suggests the four core areas, necessary to assess how the company is run from the perspective of the four main aspects of a "responsible focus:"

- **Employees.**
- **Environmental.**
- **Societal.**
- **Governance.**

The categories reflect the traditional ESG with the added aspect of additional workforce / employee information. Note that metrics must report not just on what policies the organisation has in place but the actual performance. The objective of these suggestions is to establish the material metrics, (i.e., relevant to a person needing to make a decision about a company) that apply to all companies regardless of size, location, or sector (i.e., industry agnostic).

We accept that some metrics are clearly universal, but others are open to debate. What might this ESG+1 look like?

12.1 Employee, Environmental, Social and Governance Reporting (EESG) The social report card.

This "non-financial" reporting framework should help broaden the feedback both operationally and from a governance perspective to make sure the required metrics are in place.

- It is important that employees, consumers, and investors have access to *non-financial information* about the business allowing them to assess the true culture of the organisation, risks and opportunities and the long-term sustainability of the business.
- This non-financial reporting includes information about
    - Employees: are they "good jobs?" How the organization treats its employees and how they feel about the business (especially related to abiding by the stated values and code of ethics)
    - Other workforce issues – for example, the working conditions for people working as part of the supply chain.
    - Environmental issues: how the organisation performs as a steward of nature and the environment based on facts.
    - Societal issues: how the organisation treats customers, suppliers, and communities based on factual feedback.
    - Governance: the provision of information on the company's sustainability strategy, the experience and capabilities of the leadership team, internal controls and processes, executive pay and shareholder rights.

- The EESG Report must commence with a background summary of the Company demonstrating its credentials as a responsible business, as a business that people can trust, as a company worth buying from, doing business with, working for, and investing in.
- The report must include past (where available), current and projected metrics on the key material issues affecting employees, the environment, society, and the governance of the company.
- A company's EESG report must be easily accessible to all interested stakeholders. For employees via the company's intranet/newsletters etc, for other stakeholders via the company's website and annual accounts.

This report will enable all stakeholders to assess whether the company is aware of the risks and opportunities It faces going forward, the long-term sustainability of the organisation and its status as a responsible business. It will enable them to determine whether they wish to work for, purchase from or invest in.

Who are the EESG metrics for?

A company's EESG report must be easily accessible to all interested stakeholders, i.e., via the company's intranet and / or newsletters and CSR / sustainability / impact reports in addition to the company's website and annual accounts.

Who needs this non-financial information and why might they be interested? Key "stakeholders" might include:

- **Employees:** on the company's contribution to making the world a better place
- **Investors**: on the company's future risks and opportunities and whether to invest
- **Consumers**: on whether the company is making a positive contribution to the world

Guidance on developing and using metrics.

- **Communities**: on the company's contribution to the local community
- **Government**: on whether a company is meeting its legal requirements

Organisations often form "user groups" of key stakeholders who can provide information on what information would be help.

The EESG report

The introduction to the EESG Report is vital. It will provide a lens on the company with regards to its long-term sustainability and will be of particular interest to investors, lenders, current and potential employees who will use it to determine its investability and employment prospects. The report should include:

- evidence of the Board's commitment to a responsible business strategy, a summary of this strategy and vision for the future, how it was formulated, introduced and how it will be maintained.
- a summary of the true culture of the organisation and its level of commitment to people and planet issues.
- demonstration of an understanding of the future risks and opportunities confronting the company and what appropriate action is to be taken.
- details of the company's Values and Code of Ethics, evidence that these are embedded into the company's DNA and how it plays a part in the culture of the organisation and decision-making process.
- evidence that rewards and incentives for all employees, including C-suite, will be based on the company's values, Code of Ethics, and material EESG targets.
- evidence that the company's internal management systems (governance) serve to ensure that EESG activities are

implemented at the operational level, and which permit monitoring of these activities.
- evidence that sufficient resources are available to produce these metrics and communicate them to relevant stakeholders. Explanation of where this EESG information can be found by interested parties.
- the name of the person(s) at Board Level responsible for EESG issues.
- Independent evidence to be provided wherever possible. Otherwise sign-off by a named senior executive

The following examples include both numeric metrics as well as items suggested where a narrative would be more relevant. The term "materiality" is also used. An item can be material from the viewpoint of one stakeholder (e.g., investors) or multiple stakeholders.

Note: the term "non-financial reporting" has been used but readers should remember that in all cases organisations actually spend money to make investments in developing many of these resources. So, they do impact financial information.

Reporting on employee-oriented aspects

Pay and wages	• % Of full and part-time staff not receiving at least minimum living wage • Mean pay gap % based on gender and ethnicity. • Summary of total salaries, benefits, and pensions + mean average
Employees	• Total # broken down by gender and ethnicity & region
Contract of employment	• % Of employees (full and part-time) who feel that their contract of employment is fair or very fair
Equality of opportunity	• % Of employees who believe that every employee, by age, gender, religion, ethnicity, and other groups have equal opportunities to be employed, to express their opinion and progress.
Safety, Health, and wellbeing	• % Of employees who feel their company is concerned or very concerned about their mental, physical, and financial wellbeing and acts where necessary • Absentee rate through ill-health in previous and current years. Average # days p.a. • % reported incidents where injury occurred per 1,000 people
Diversity and inclusion	• Describe the process that leads to a diverse workforce. • % Of employees who believe that the Company is inclusive
Speak up and whistleblowing	• % Of employees who believe there are fair and effective processes for speaking up and whistleblowing
Training	• Amount of training £ per full time employee • Total £ for all employees

Several of the line-item metrics shown will be familiar and represent traditional reporting (e.g., safety incident reporting). However, note that several would be extracted from an employee feedback approach – a regular "flash" report, or a regular short series of either consistent or varied questions.

The important aspect that it is a representation of employee opinions rather than a numerical count or statistic.

Reporting on environment related aspects

Greenhouse Gas Emissions (GHG)	• # Metric tonnes of CO2 equivalent – Scope 1 and 2 • Set target(s) for net-zero GHG emissions
Electricity consumption	• % Of electricity consumed from renewable resources – Set targets for 100% renewable
Waste and wastewater management	• # Of metric tonnes/person employed. • Set targets
Air travel on company business	• Average miles/person employed travelling by air i.e., the total number of miles travelled divided by # of employees. • Set targets
Car travel on company business	• Average miles/person employed travelling by car
Journeys to and from work	• The total number of miles travelled by car divided by # of employees. • Set targets. • Outline incentives which encourage employees to travel by public transport or car-share

Note that the metrics are expanded from the traditional consumption, output and outcome targets related to operational activity and include environmental impacts that the organization has, based on its location, work policies etc., that create a societal impact on the environment.

Also note that clear targets should be established for several metrics and that in some areas commentary / narrative should also be added.

Reporting on social (community, society) related aspects

Contribution to society (CTS)	• # Employees by age group, gender, locality, and other indicators: by region • Total tax collected showing income and corporation tax, other employee related taxes, vat, property tax. • Community investment in £'s: by region
Social purpose (SP)	• Outline the Company's social purpose(s), why this SP was chosen, the total social investment (£), the impact on society and/or the planet: including, • Pro bono investment # hours and total value
Stakeholder engagement	• Outline process for engaging on EESG issues with material stakeholders (customers, suppliers, local communities, shareholders)
Quality of products and services	• Evidence that quality, healthy, safe, and sustainable products, and services are prioritised and being introduced with target dates
Transparent and ethical sales and marketing	• Evidence that this theme is prioritised
Customer privacy and data security	• Summary of the management strategy regarding risk to customer and user data

Many of these suggested reporting items are narrative based. Users may be looking to see that an organisation has addressed certain aspects of "social responsibility and accountability" even if there are no "standard" metrics that might be used.

Some areas might also overlap with other reporting – as an example the levels of tax paid must link back to financial reporting. In some cases, items being reported may also require evidence of adherence to legal requirements e.g., data privacy.

Guidance on developing and using metrics.

Reporting of governance related aspects

Corporate purpose	• Describe the company's purpose and how it is embedded into its DNA
Composition and quality of the governing body	• Total members: executive and non- executive, details of experience
Remuneration policy for senior executives	• Provide details and state how the policy connects to the company's purpose and long-term value, particularly incentives
Company Values and Code of Ethics	• Summarise the Company's values and Code of Ethics, state how they were formulated and how they are integrated into Company decision-making
Governance	• Provide evidence that the internal management systems serve to ensure the law is not broken and EESG activities are implemented at operational level.
Investment policy	• Define the company's investment policy with metrics
Employee representation	• Summarise the evidence that employees' voices are heard at Board Level
Risks and opportunities	• Summarise the company's views on the material risks and opportunities facing the company (i.e. societal, economic and environmental risks) and what appropriate action is to be taken.
Rewards and incentives	• Provide details of the rewards and incentives schemes based on non-financial targets.
Who is responsible for EESG metrics	• Name the person(s) and job title(s) and position, affirming their responsibility for accuracy

It is recognized that several of these items might be considered "commercially confidential" and that is a challenge that organisations will need to assess during their deliberations on how much can be disclosed.

Again, certain suggested aspects may already be included in existing notes to financial reporting such as director / executive compensation.

The idea of using these four EESG metrics is provided more as a "thinking exercise" that a suggested list of items to just be adopted and reported. The most important question that a Responsible Business will be asked will be:

- ***"As an employee, or prospective employee what would I like to know about this business and how it operates"*** or
- ***"As an investor what added information would I like to be aware of that allows me to more effectively understand company performance, risk and sustainability?"***

Corporate reporting can be viewed in two ways. Either as a compliance exercise where only the mandatory information is provided, or as a "story telling exercise." In this approach, an organization provides enough information to support its claim to be a Responsible Business.

Two significant issues exist.

Firstly, all data and information provided takes time and effort to produce and there must be a clear benefit to creating the report.

Second, many organisations do in fact try and use corporate reporting as storytelling – but the stories don't always tell the full story or the whole truth. This is where the problem of "green washing" (or social washing or other names) comes into play. Extreme damage can be done to the integrity and credibility of an organisation when it tells a good story which turns out not to be true. (See more discussion on "washing" issues in section 12.3).

This is why we recommend that an independent opinion on these metrics is provided wherever possible. Otherwise, the metrics need to be signed off by a named senior executive. Ideally both would be better.

Corporate reporting is a moving target at the present time. Do not be afraid to go slowly and experiment.

12.2   Links to ESG and other reporting

This book would not be complete without some type of link back to the many emerging approaches to corporate accountability that have developed over the past half century and continue to evolve. ESG is the "current state of the art" standing for Environment, Social and Governance. This approach has evolved over more than twenty years. ESG is currently the object of some level of concern and pushback related to complexity, inconsistency, incompleteness, and lack of comparability.

We believe that Responsible Business transcends much of the content of these approaches and frameworks. The Responsible Business approach is holistic and sees the business as an integrated system both internally as well as within society. Operating as a Responsible Business should address many of the concerns driving calls for greater accountability through establishing a culture that is caring in all aspects.

Corporate reporting has traditionally focused on compliance reporting. A large component of this has been the reporting to investors on financial information. This has been supplemented over the years by requirements for supplemental reporting by various financial organizations that regulate the financial marketplace such as the Financial Reporting Council (FRC) in the UK and the Securities and Exchange Commission (SEC) in the US. Additional information is often also required by legislation governing business such as the several types of Companies Acts and their equivalents.

Societal concern is driving accountability and reporting.

The drive for greater transparency and accountability by business has been a theme for many years. As mentioned earlier J&J developed their "credo" for business in 1943 that started with a greater recognition of their social responsibility.

Global changes further accelerated this journey. Accounting records based on historic valuations of property became increasingly misleading as inflation took hold starting in the 1970's. Globalization, especially the development of global supply chains involving out-sourcing to less developed nations resulted in major social scandals and problems in the 1970's and 1980's related to issues such as dangerous workplaces, and child labour.

Ethical scandals and increasingly visible global ethical issues (often rapidly revealed because of the growth of the internet and social media), seemed to rapidly expand in the 1980's. The Savings and Loan scandals in the US. Plundering of pensions funds in the UK as well as events like the Bank of Credit and Commerce International (ICCS).

Several responses were voluntary, for example the development of a Standard for Social Accountability Certification (SA 8000), followed by an International Standard on guidance for Social Responsibility (ISO 26000). Some large purchasers required certification to these standards from suppliers, as a condition of supply.

In the 1990's the environmental movement took hold with various UN committees and publications as well as regional and national responses. The ISO 14000 series of environmental standards were released. These were followed by a series of studies and international meetings that eventually led to the (general) acceptance that global warming was a critical problem.

The term "externalities" became popular as it was quickly recognized that many businesses were impacting natural resources, to the detriment of society and the planet, but had no incentive to take action as they incurred no cost of this exploitation. These were "externalities" for which business did not pay. This included the use of all the various services that society paid for through government resources, for example roads, education, and social services. (Also clean up's, spills, waste, remediation and others).

Governments started to introduce legislation around emissions and investors began to realize that down the road there may be financial penalties if business continued to ignore externalities, so the call for greater disclosure started to grow.

Various frameworks and models began to develop to allow for broader based corporate reporting with a heavy emphasis on the environment. The Global Reporting Initiative (GRI) guidelines developed as one of the leading frameworks but once again adoption was and remains voluntary.

The concept of integrated thinking

In parallel to the general concerns about business conduct in particular the high-profile issue of the environment, business itself was changing. The service economy started to grow, which was accelerated by the technological developments that took place after the 1980's. Computerization, high-speed, low-cost communications together with the growth of the internet brought substantial improvement in data sharing and information availability.

Organisations recognized that people were no longer required to operate machines but were hired for their brain power – their intellectual capital. People were moving from a perceived belief of being "inter-changeable" and a quickly replaced commodity, to being an "asset" – something that brings operational capacity and has value. This led to major changes in working conditions with organisations investing more in people related areas, and providing many types of incentives, inducements, and facilities to attract and retain staff. The "knowledge economy" had arrived.

These changes led to a growing concern that financial "capital" remained important but that other "capitals" were also critical in terms of building an organisations business model. The term human capital was adopted and applied to the workforce, and this was combined with the "free" capital not being paid for and included in externalities. (Interesting that the core components within this early framework reflected people, planet, and profit).

A movement began to re-position corporate reporting and accountability around the broader concept of multiple capitals. While financial reporting remained essential, investors, regulators and others started to ask about the activities and risks associated with these other capitals. One of the leaders at the time was the UK Association of Chartered Certified Accountants (ACCA), who worked with other UK bodies to create a "new" multi-capital reporting framework. The program was called the SIGMA project and proposed five capitals – financial, natural, social, human, and manufactured.

One of the main benefits from this model was the strengthening of the reality that business operated as an integrated (holistic) model. While decision making traditionally was heavily weighted to address financial outcomes, there was a growing realization that this focus was often resulting in maximizing financial performance but creating unseen and unreported impacts on other "capitals."

What evolved was integrated thinking – the firming up of the reality of the cause-and-effect impact of decision making in business and the importance of considering the interest of not only investors – providers of the financial capital, but of others. People - both as employees and others within the social framework that a business impacts, and the planet, where the impact was realized to be potentially global.

While these other critical resources were growing in importance, the amounts being invested were not disclosed. This problem gradually led to financial reporting providing less insight into organisational health and its ability to be a "going concern." This led to a growing discrepancy between the market or economic value of a business and its accounting value.

The "integration" of reporting

In 2009, the HRH the Prince of Wales convened a high-level meeting of investors, standard setters, companies, accounting bodies and UN representatives including The Prince's Accounting for Sustainability Project, International Federation of Accountants (IFAC), and the Global Reporting Initiative (GRI), to establish the International Integrated Reporting Committee (IIRC), a body to oversee the creation of a globally accepted Integrated Reporting framework.

In November 2011, the Committee was renamed the International Integrated Reporting Council. In 2013 the IIRC issued its proposed framework of reporting that identified six capitals – financial, natural, social and relationship, human, intellectual, and manufactured (similar to the capitals identified in the SIGMA project). These covered the core resources that were needed in most business models.

This proposed reporting framework was then applied on a voluntary basis by various organisations globally to test its value and viability. Meanwhile further voluntary frameworks were being expanded and developed and various regulators were starting to respond to societal pressure for greater disclosure.

A problem was also starting to develop around the burden of this added reporting. The inconsistency across national boundaries and its lack of consistent adoption made comparative assessments between organisations and within sectors extremely difficult for those using the reports.

By 2020 there was a major re-organisation of the various bodies developing corporate reporting models. The IIRC – the creator of integrated reporting was merged with the US based Sustainability Accounting Standards Board (SASB), into a new organisation called the VRF (Value Reporting Foundation). SASB, particularly in the US had become the de facto foundation for reporting non-financial information, principally environmentally related aspects.

This appeared to be a positive move but clearly left financial reporting outside. If true integration and single format reporting was to be achieved somehow the "accounting folks" would have to be at the party. This realization led to the consolidation of the VRF into the IFRS Foundation (International Reporting Standards Board) in 2022.

> The IFRS Foundation is a not-for-profit, public interest organisation established to develop high-quality, understandable, enforceable and globally accepted accounting and sustainability disclosure standards.
>
> Our Standards are developed by our two standard-setting boards, the International Accounting Standards Board (IASB) and International Sustainability Standards Board (ISSB).

Through this amalgamation the International Standards for both financial reporting and the non-financial aspects through the ISSB are brought together. The ISSB is currently in deliberation about release of its first standards.

A challenge remains that, apart from these international standards, there remain other mandatory reporting requirements. Those required by legal statute that vary by country, including those demanded by various financial securities bodies like the SEC. Additionally organisations like the European Union have already introduced broad based supplemental reporting standards.

The EU Corporate Sustainability Reporting Directive (CSRD), introduce more detailed reporting requirements on companies' impact on the environment, human rights, and social standards, based on common criteria in line with EU's climate goals. The Commission will adopt the first set of standards by June 2023.

Not only have these standards been issued ahead of the ISSB requirements, but they also appear to be more detailed than those expected once the initial ISSB requirements are released. Another key difference is that the EU has adopted a process whereby organisations reporting will have to consider materiality from the perspective of ALL stakeholders, whereas indications are that the ISSB will be adopting the traditional accounting view of assessing materiality from an investor viewpoint.

To ensure companies are providing reliable information, the EU requirements will be subject to independent auditing and certification. Financial and sustainability reporting will be on an equal footing, and investors will have comparable and reliable data. Digital access to sustainability information will also have to be guaranteed.

So, the whole approach to corporate reporting remains in evolution.

12.3   A new "whole system" measure

One challenge in assessing business performance has been to select a metric that provides a concise snapshot of overall results. For many years the measurement of profit has been such a measure. Everything pulled together in a single number.

But a problem has been developing over the years. While profit is a good measure of financial outcomes, financial capital – while remaining important, Is now more of an enabler than the principal ingredient. What profit fails to show is what is happening with the underlying aspects of the organisation and its' business model. Users may have been lulled into thinking that as long as an organisation was profitable, all was well.

An organisation named The Maturity Institute came to the conclusion that a new, more holistic measure was required. The Institute spent many years developing and validating its' approach to measuring total organisation performance. Its' measure of what is called organisational maturity, or OMINDEX©, is obtained through an assessment process that looks at many factors considered critical to the health, sustainability and well being of an organisation. It measures its' level of maturity. This is its' ability to effectively bring together a holistic business that achieves both sustainable performance that is people-centric. It states that:

MI's purpose is to maximise the creation of Total Stakeholder Value (TSV), which incorporates both company performance and societal value.

More detail is available from the website and the company. Each organisation can be individually assessed as to its' maturity and the overall results are expressed in a metric based on the scale used by S&P for credit ratings.

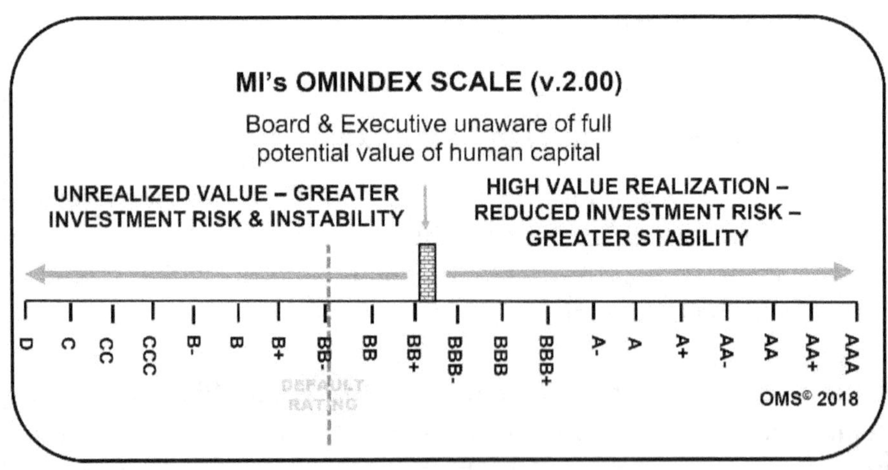

Research demonstrates that to be a mature organisation, a rating of between BB+ and BBB would be expected. Below this, an organisation is being sub-optimised. Above this there starts to be realised the opportunities for enhanced performance.

As can be seen, the average benchmark of those assessed to date is around BB- indicating lots of opportunity for improvement.

Other versions of the chart demonstrate how an organisations risk profile varies at different scores. Such a rating would provide a solid advance on assurances provided by an audit report, that an organisation is considered sustainable as a "going concern." Clearly, based on evidence such as Carillion in the UK, a "clean" audit report does not provide such an assurance!

The OMINDEX rating provides a very solid step forward in assessing the health and quality of an integrated business model, and its ability to create and sustain value.

12.4   Concerns over green-washing and other illusions

Greater transparency and disclosure are great – but is the information always accurate and honest? Greenwashing is when the management team within an organisation and / or those responsible for governance such as the board, make and approve false, unsubstantiated, or outright misleading statements or claims relating to the sustainability of-its business operations or related to its products or services.

Some greenwashing may be unintentional, due to a lack of knowledge or understanding, but sometimes greenwashing is also conducted intentionally through marketing efforts, focused on "good PR." In chapter nine, "The case for change" we included an example of the Mobil / Exxon knowledge of climate change, where their response appears to have been to hire PR experts to "spin the story."

Early definitions of Greenwashing revolved mostly around environmental claims. With the evolution of Environmental, Social & Governance (ESG) disclosure, the market's understanding and interpretation of "sustainability" has expanded to include Social and Governance factors as well.

As such, greenwashing activity may now include statements that extend beyond just environmental claims. This term has recently been expanded by the UK body Planet Tracker in a report "Greenwashing Hydra." This new report warns of six types of greenwashing from corporates."

- "Greencrowding" built on the notion that hiding amongst a "crowd" of other corporates can keep environmentally damaging approaches hidden. (Such as claiming involvement in an industry improvement approach but not doing anything individually).
- "Greenlighting" describes how companies shine a spotlight on green credentials to draw attention away from environmentally damaging activities. Focusing on what we are doing and ignoring all else. Often called "telling the truth attractively" yet having major omissions.
- "Greenshifting" refers to when companies try and shift the blame up or down the value chain, usually toward consumers.
- "Greenlabelling" is a practice where marketing departments mislead through their adverts by claiming something is green.
- "Greenrinsing," when companies regularly change climate and sustainability targets before they've been achieved.
- "Greenhushing" refers to corporates under-reporting or even hiding their sustainability data and performance to avoid stakeholder scrutiny.

These are all sad side effects from a lack of honesty and integrity. Eventually organisations will be "found out" as problems will surface at some point. Maybe after the current CEO has moved on. The root cause of the problem is irresponsible decision making.

Certification of compliance and good conduct is one avenue to organizations that want to work towards a better future. Certified "B Corps" are an example.

Guidance on developing and using metrics.

According to their website, and supported by many notable organizations, Certified B Corporations are leaders in the global movement for an inclusive, equitable, and regenerative economy. Unlike other certifications for businesses, B Lab is unique in their ability to measure a company's entire social and environmental impact. The following is quoted from the B Corp website:

B Corp Certification is a designation that a business is meeting high standards of verified performance, accountability, and transparency on factors from employee benefits and charitable giving to supply chain practices and input materials. To achieve certification, a company must:

- *Demonstrate high social and environmental performance by achieving a B Impact Assessment score of 80 or above and passing our risk review. Multinational corporations must also meet baseline requirement standards.*
- *Make a legal commitment by changing their corporate governance structure to be accountable to all stakeholders, not just shareholders, and achieve benefit corporation status if available in their jurisdiction.*
- *Exhibit transparency by allowing information about their performance measured against B Lab's standards to be publicly available on their B Corp profile on B Lab's website.*

As leaders in the movement for economic systems change, B Corps reap remarkable benefits. They build trust with consumers, communities, and suppliers; attract and retain employees; and draw mission-aligned investors. As they are required to undergo the verification process every three years to recertify, B Corps are also focused on continuous improvement, leading to their long-term resiliency.

Responsible business as a foundation for corporate accountability

This book has presented an argument that a Responsible Business is built around a comprehensive approach that focuses on all key stakeholders. The Responsible Business represents a "way of thinking and operating" that seeks to balance a wide range of multiple interests including those of an investor who requires a return on their investment (ROI).

Investors also want some level of "safety" for their investment. Annual audits and internal control systems are part of the assurance that provides insight into risks an organisation may have in both complying with legal requirements and also, importantly, being able to sustain itself as a "going concern."

Boards and management have a responsibility to ensure that their approaches to strategy and operations are both commercially and societally focused on purpose. This requires that they build into their planning an awareness with current realities within society (often achieved by the environmental scan used in planning).

The world is changing, and organisations need to be "fit for purpose" in terms of aligning with both market expectations as well as social "norms." Sustainability has developed as the buzzword for addressing some of these changes in the method of planning and operating. Some organizations have hired somebody to head up their "sustainability" activities. Here is an example of what a job in sustainability represents according to the University of Wisconsin.

> **What tools and skills does a sustainability manager need?**
>
> Sustainable business leaders use a range of skills to achieve their goals. While commonalities exist across the board, specific tools and skills will vary depending on the industry. First and foremost, sustainability professionals must be able to solve complex business problems by practicing systems thinking—analyzing whole systems by understanding how component parts interact with each other. They also must understand basic principles of economics, marketing, and accounting, as well as how to assess and interpret social, scientific, and business-related information.

Our belief, hopefully explained in this book, is that sustainability and responding to changes in the market is an organisational issue. We do not believe another department is needed. Responding to the changes is an organisational wide change in the way of doing business. Building a plan, do, check, and act management model on the pillars and foundations of a Responsible Business. It is a whole system "way of doing business."

It is, in fact all about the culture. About how we do business around here. Every day. Day in. Day out.

Guidance on developing and using metrics.

13 Appendices

List of Appendices

13.1   Sample Champion commitment agreement

13.2   Memo from the Board to all employees

Responsible Business Champion Commitment

I believe that the business sector, and very specifically, the people working within this community, have a responsibility towards people and the planet as well as making an ethical profit.

As a Responsible Business Champion, I will actively promote responsible business within my organisation and make a personal commitment, within my sphere of influence, to help make it commonplace by 2030. I will challenge irresponsible behaviour and decision-making when I see it and I will urge my colleagues and connections to do likewise.

As a Responsible Business Champion I agree, to the best of my ability and within my sphere of influence, to adhere to the following:

With regards to People
I will endeavour to ensure a great workplace culture where all decisions and behaviours are based on the company's **Values** and **Code of Ethics**, a workplace where all our people enjoy their work, are fairly paid, engaged, well-trained, physically, and psychologically safe, have equal opportunities and enjoy a great life balance.

I will help build the company's **social purpose** – how the company can make the world a better place.

I will not undertake, nor ask a colleague to undertake, any illegal or unethical behaviour.

With regards to the Planet
I will consider the **ethical implications,** as well as legal, of all my decisions and work practices which have an environmental impact.

Responsible Business.

I will collaborate with colleagues and other key stakeholders to develop and improve our Company's positive contribution to the environmental.

I will play my part in ensuring and maintaining environmental management, measurement and reporting systems that provide the framework needed to embed environmental considerations into our culture.

With regards to our corporate aims and objectives
I will play my part, within my sphere of influence, in meeting my Company's financial aims and objectives via an ethical, **socially responsible,** and environmentally sustainable business strategy.

Signed:

Note that in the draft document above several terms were used – values, code of ethics, social purpose. Depending upon the maturity of the organizations journey some of these items may not yet be in place – and may be part of the deliverables within the goals and objectives of the culture change team. The wording of the commitment statement must reflect the reality of what is currently in place.

Responsible Business.

A Memo from the Board to all Employees

Dear Colleague,

We aspire to be a Responsible Business
Alongside you all, we want "our business" to play its part in resolving some of the problems facing our society and the world. With this objective in mind, we are embarking on a significant culture change programme enabling us to play our part as a Responsible Business. **We want you all to be involved in its creation.**

As a good corporate citizen, our strategy, with your help, is to be a Responsible Business giving priority equally to people, planet, and profit (and other commercial objectives) where:

- Our decision-making, focussing on doing no harm, is firmly embedded into our DNA through our company values and Code of Ethics.
- Where we treat ourselves and others decently and respectfully.
- We all have good jobs, feel valued and empowered and work in a safe and inclusive environment that prioritises good mental physical and moral well-being.
- We will reduce and eventually eliminate our negative impact on the climate and the environment by setting bold and ambitious targets, meeting these targets, and encouraging and incentivising all our stakeholders to do likewise.
- We have fair and transparent processes of governance based on fair pay and equal opportunities for all.
- We are encouraged and enabled to thrive and lead a balanced life.
- We all feel that our jobs have a social purpose which contributes to the well-being of the world.

This process, which will begin immediately, will be supported morally and financially by the Board, will be people-centric and involve everyone who wishes to contribute to the process.

Signed by the CEO and Members of the Board.

Responsible Business.

Responsible Business.

14 References

Note that the website references were valid at the time of publications but may change. Books have also been included in the bibliography as an alternative reference.

14.1   Examples of Codes of Ethics

3M https://www.3m.com/3M/en_US/ethics-compliance/code/

Amazon https://ir.aboutamazon.com/corporate-governance/documents-and-charters/code-of-business-conduct-and-ethics/default.aspx

Enron https://bobsutton.typepad.com/files/enron-ethics.pdf - Important - see https://www.investopedia.com/updates/enron-scandal-summary/ for further information.

Ethical Reading
https://www.ethicalreading.org.uk/programmes/business-ethics-and-culture/our-code-of-ethics/

Shell https://www.shell.com/about-us/our-values/code-of-ethics.html

Responsible Business.

14.2   Other organisations promoting ethics and values.

The Institute of Business Ethics: promotes high standards of business behaviour based on ethical values. https://www.ibe.org.uk/

Business in the Community; connecting responsible businesses throughout the UK. https://www.bitc.org.uk/

Good Business Charter: gives accreditation to businesses that promote and
implement ethical policies. https://www.goodbusinesscharter.com/

Blueprint for Better Business; Uniting Corporate Purpose and Personal Values to Serve Society. https://www.blueprintforbusiness.org/

B Corps UK: Certified B Corps are a new kind of business that balances purpose and profit. https://bcorporation.uk/

CIPD: The professional body for HR and People Development
https://www.cipd.co.uk/

Ethical Reading: helping businesses in Reading do the right thing by each other, the community, and the environment.
https://www.ethicalreading.org.uk/

Eat Sleep Work Repeat: A podcast about making work better.
https://eatsleepworkrepeat.com/

HRD Direct: A resource for HR Directors and Senior HR Practitioners.
https://www.thehrdirector.com/

Behavioural Ethics – Ethics unwrapped: McCombs School of Business
https://ethicsunwrapped.utexas.edu/glossary/behavioral-ethics

Responsible Business.

Responsible Business.

14.3 Mental Health Resources

Mental Health First Aid (Training course) https://mhfaengland.org/
MIND https://www.mind.org.uk/workplace/mental-health-at-work/
- Taking Care of Yourself
  https://www.mind.org.uk/workplace/mental-health-at-work/taking-care-of-yourself/
- Taking Care of your staff
  https://www.mind.org.uk/workplace/mental-health-at-work/taking-care-of-your-staff/
- Training and consultancy
  https://www.mind.org.uk/workplace/training-consultancy/
- A-Z of Mental Health https://www.mind.org.uk/information-support/a-z-mental-health/
- Know your rights https://www.mind.org.uk/information-support/legal-rights/discrimination-at-work/overview/
- How do deal with stigma https://www.mind.org.uk/information-support/legal-rights/

Acas (The Advisory, Conciliation and Arbitration Service) https://www.acas.org.uk/

Stress Management Society https://www.stress.org.uk/

Business in the Community (BITC) BITC has produced a *Mental Health Toolkit for Employers*. This offers a range of free resources and will help you to formulate an action plan https://www.bitc.org.uk/toolkit/mental-health-for-employers-toolkit/

Responsible Business.

14.4   Physical and Financial Health Resources

Physical Health
NICE: Promoting Physical Health in the Workplace
https://www.nice.org.uk/guidance/ph13/chapter/1-Recommendations

National Health Scotland: Promoting Physical Health in the Workplace
https://www.healthyworkinglives.scot/resources/publications/Documents
/promoting-physical-activity-in-the-workplace.pdf

MindTools: Improving Physical Health in the Workplace
https://www.mindtools.com/pages/article/health-and-well-being.htm
USA

Sport England: How physical activity helps Mental Health;
https://www.sportengland.org/campaigns-and-our-work/mental-health

Financial Health

CIPD: Financial Well-being in the workplace
https://www.cipd.co.uk/knowledge/culture/well-being/employee-
financial-well-being

Money and Mental Health Institute: Best practice for Employers
https://www.moneyandmentalhealth.org/wp-
content/uploads/2018/05/Best-practice-checklist-Employers.pdf

Further Reading on Employee Surveys

Some useful comments about employee surveys <u>6 Mistakes Companies Make with Employee Surveys (workhuman.com)</u>

Ethics at Work: 2021 international survey of employees from The Institute of Business <u>Ethics at Work: 2021 International Survey of Employees | Institute of Business Ethics – IBE</u>

13 Key Aspects To Consider When Selecting An Employee Engagement Survey Tool by Forbes <u>13 Key Aspects To Consider When Selecting An Employee Engagement Survey Tool (forbes.com)</u>

How to Run a Focus Group for Your Business <u>How to Run a Focus Group for Your Business (hubspot.com)</u>

Responsible Business.

14.5   Useful reading: Culture and Purpose

Corporate Culture: Combining Purpose and Values and how poor culture can stifle creativity and success and how to fix it by Nick Shepherd. https://www.waterstones.com/book/corporate-culture-combining-purpose-and-values/nick-a-shepherd/9781777570323

Corporate Purpose: Why it matters more than strategy by Shankar Basu. https://blackwells.co.uk/bookshop/product/Corporate-Purpose-by-Shankar-Basu-author/9781138056534

Everybody Matters: The Extraordinary Power of caring for your People like Family by Bob Chapman and Raj Sisodia. https://www.barrywehmiller.com/outreach/book

Excellence Now: Extreme Humanism by Tom Peters. https://www.goodreads.com/en/book/show/56462783-excellence-now

Giving Vices to Values: How to speak your mind when you know what's right by Mary C Gentile. https://books.google.co.uk/books/about/Giving_Voice_to_Values.html?id=4H8wEAAAQBAJ&source=kp_book_description&redir_esc=y

Holacracy: The Revolutionary Management System that abolishes Hierarchy by Brian J. Robertson. http://holacracybook.com/

Intentional Integrity: How smart companies can lead the ethical revolution by Robert Chestnut. https://www.intentionalintegrity.com/

Servant Leadership: A journey into the nature of legitimate power and greatness by Robert K.

Responsible Business.

Greenleaf.https://www.goodreads.com/en/book/show/181737.Servant_L
eadership

Speak Up: The how to guide to navigating the power and politics of conversations at work by Megan Reitz and John Higgins.
https://www.meganreitz.com/speakup/How

The Cost of Poor Culture: The massive financial opportunity in an enhanced workplace climate by Nick A. Shepherd.
https://www.waterstones.com/book/the-cost-of-poor-culture/nick-a-shepherd//9781777570347

The Good Jobs Strategy: How the smartest companies invest in employees to lower costs and boost profits by Zeynep Ton.
https://www.goodreads.com/book/show/17346828-the-good-jobs-strategy

The Intrapreneur: Confessions of a corporate insurgent by Gib Bulloch.
https://gibbulloch.com/2018/

The Joy of Work: 30 ways to fall in love with your job again by Bruce Daisley. https://eatsleepworkrepeat.com/

The Purpose Economy: How your desire for impact, personal growth and community is changing the world.https://www.goodreads.com/book/show/18089375-the-purpose-economy-how-your-desire-for-impact-personal-growth-and-com

The Serendipity Mindset: The art and science of creating good luck by Dr Christian Busch. https://theserendipitymindset.com/

14.6 Progressive Capitalism

Dying for a Paycheck: How modern management harms employee health and company performance– and what we can do about it by Jeffrey Pfeffert. https://jeffreypfeffer.com/books/dying-for-a-paycheck/

Everybody's Business: The unlikely story of how big business can fix the world by Jon Miller and Lucy Parker. https://www.waterstones.com/book/everybodys-business/lucy-parker/jon-miller/9781849546089

Green Swans: the coming boom in regenerative capitalism by John Elkington. https://volans.com/project/green-swans/

Grow the Pie: How Great Companies Deliver Both Purpose and Profit by Alex Edmans. https://www.growthepie.net/

How Good Can We Be: Ending the mercenary society and building a great country by Will Hutton. https://www.hachette.co.uk/titles/will-hutton/how-good-we-can-be/9780349140087/

Impact: reshaping capitalism to drive real change by Sir Ronald Cohen. https://sirronaldcohen.org/booksIntentional

People, Planet and Profit: how to embrace sustainability for innovation and business growth by Peter Fisk. https://www.goodreads.com/en/book/show/7691406-people-planet-profit

Progressive Capitalism: How to achieve economic growth, liberty, and social justice by David Sainsbury.

Responsible Business.

https://www.waterstones.com/book/progressive-capitalism/david-sainsbury/9781849545297

Reinventing Organizations: a guide to creating organisations inspired by the next stage of human consciousness by Frederic Laloux. https://www.reinventingorganizations.com/

Rotten: Why corporate misconduct continues and what to do about it by Marc J. Epstein and Kirk O. Hanson. https://www.waterstones.com/book/rotten/marc-j-epstein/kirk-o-hanson/9781735336114

The Breakthrough Challenge: 10 ways to connect today's profits with tomorrows bottom line by John Elkington and Jochen Zeitz. https://www.goodreads.com/book/show/23444840-the-breakthrough-challenge

The Ethical Capitalist: How to make business work better for society by Julian Richer. https://www.waterstones.com/book/the-ethical-capitalist-how-to-make-business-work-better-for-society/julian-richer/9781847942210

The Future of Capitalism: Facing the New Anxieties by Paul Collier. https://www.goodreads.com/book/show/36628413-the-future-of-capitalism

The Responsibility Revolution: How the next generation of businesses will win by Jeffrey Hollender and Bill Breen. https://www.goodreads.com/book/show/6628285-the-responsibility-revolution

Responsible Business.

The Way Out: kick-starting capitalism to save our economic arse by L Hunter Lovins and Boyd Cohen.
https://www.goodreads.com/book/show/12510825-the-way-out

Welcome to GoodCo: Using the tools of business to create public good by Tom Levitt. https://www.goodreads.com/book/show/21994453-welcome-to-goodco

Responsible Business.

14.7   Environmental Issues

Business and Environmental Sustainability: Foundations, challenges, and corporate functions by Sigran M Wagner.
https://books.google.co.uk/books/about/Business_and_Environmental_S
ustainabilit.html?id=vaHsDwAAQBAJ&redir_esc=y

Cradle to Cradle: Remaking the way we make things Michael Braungart and William McDonough.
https://www.betterworldbooks.com/search/results?q=0865475873

Doughnut Economics: seven ways to think like a 21st Century economist by Kate Raworth. https://www.waterstones.com/book/doughnut-economics/kate-raworth/9781847941398

Drawdown: the most comprehensive plan ever proposed to reverse global warming by Paul Hawken.
https://www.waterstones.com/book/drawdown/paul-hawken/9780141988436

Ecology of Commerce: a declaration of sustainability by Paul Hawken.
https://www.betterworldbooks.com/search/results?q=0887307043

How to Avoid a Climate Disaster: the solutions we have and the breakthroughs we need by Bill Gates.
https://www.waterstones.com/book/how-to-avoid-a-climate-disaster/bill-gates/9780241448304

Strategy for Sustainability: a business manifesto by Adam Werbach.
https://books.google.co.uk/books/about/Strategy_for_Sustainability.html?id=-8IdGJ20XzEC

Responsible Business.

Sustainable Business: key issues by Helen Kopnina and John Blewitt. https://www.google.co.uk/books/edition/Sustainable_Business/fUxWDw AAQBAJ?hl=en&gbpv=1&dq=sustainable+business+key+issues&printsec=f rontcover

The Green to Gold Business Playbook: how to implement sustainability practices for bottom-line results in every business by function by Daniel C. Esty and P. J. Simmons. https://blackwells.co.uk/bookshop/product/The-Green-to-Gold-Business-Playbook-by-Daniel-C-Esty-P-J-Simmons/9780470590751

There is no planet B: a handbook for the make or break years by Mike Berners-Lee. https://www.waterstones.com/book/there-is-no-planet-b/mike-berners-lee/9781108821575

This Changes Everything: capitalism vs the climate by Naomi Klein. https://www.waterstones.com/book/this-changes-everything/naomi-klein/9780241956182

14.8 Corporate Governance

Financial Reporting Council Corporate Culture and the Role of Boards
Corporate Culture and the Role of Boards (frc.org.uk)

Boards that Lead: when to take charge, when to partner and when to say out of the way by Ram Charan, Dennis Carey, and Michael Useem.
https://www.goodreads.com/book/show/17675452-boards-that-lead

Corporate Governance: principles, policies and practices by Bob Tricker.
HTTPS://www.goodreads.com/book/show/55394682-corporate-governance-4e

Corporate Governance Unlocked by Alison Dillon Kibirige and Winifred Tarinyeba Kiryabwire. https://www.cgi.org.uk/shop/books/corporate-governance-unlocked

Corporate Governance: A summary of good practice by The Institute of Business Ethics. https://www.ibe.org.uk/knowledge-hub/corporate-governance.html

How Boards Work: and how they can work better in a chaotic world by Dambisa Moyo. https://www.goodreads.com/en/book/show/55277904-how-boards-work

The Essential Book of Corporate Governance by G.N. Bajpai
tps://www.waterstones.com/book/the-essential-book-of-corporate-governance/g-n-bajpai/9789385985218

Responsible Business.

15 Bibliography

Bajpai. G. N., (2016), *"The Essential Book of Corporate Governance,"* Sage Publications Pvt. Ltd.

Basu, Shankar, (2019), *"Corporate Purpose: Why It Matters More Than Strategy, "*Routledge Library Editions: The Automobile Industry)

Berners-Lee, Mike., (2021), *"There is no planet B: a handbook for the make-or-break years,"* Cambridge University Press.

Braungart, Michael., & McDonough, William., (2009), *"Cradle to Cradle: Remaking the way we make things,"* Vintage.

Bulloch, Gib., (2018), *"The Intrapreneur: Confessions of a corporate insurgent,"* Unbound Digital

Busch, Dr. Christian., (2022), *"Connect the Dots: The art and science of creating good luck,"* Penguin Life

Chapman, Bob., Sisodia, Raj. (2016), *"Everybody Matters: The Extraordinary Power of caring for your People like Family,"* Penguin Books

Charan, Ram., Carey, Dennis., & Useem, Michael., (2013), *"Boards that Lead: when to take charge, when to partner and when to say out of the way,"* Harvard Business Review Press.

Responsible Business.

Chen, Sir. Ronald., (2020), *"Impact: reshaping capitalism to drive real change,"* Ebury Press.

Chesnut, Robert., (2021), *"Intentional Integrity: How smart companies can lead the ethical revolution,"* Pan, Main Market Edition

Collier, Paul., (2019), *"The Future of Capitalism: Facing the New Anxieties,"* Penguin.

Daisley, Bruce., (2020), *"The Joy of Work: 30 ways to fix your work culture and fall in love with your job again,"* Random House Business.
Edmans, Alex., (2021), *"Grow the Pie: How Great Companies Deliver Both Purpose and Profit,"* Cambridge University Press

Elkington. John., (2021), *"Green Swans: the coming boom in regenerative capitalism,"* Fast Company Press

Elkington, John., & Zeitz, Jochen., (2014), *"The Breakthrough Challenge: 10 ways to connect today's profits with tomorrows bottom line,"* Jossey-Bass.

Epstein, Marc. J., & Hanson, Kirk. O., (2020), *"Rotten: Why corporate misconduct continues and what to do about it,"* Lanark Press.

Esty Daniel. C., & Simmons. P. J., (2011), *"The Green to Gold Business Playbook: how to implement sustainability practices for bottom-line results in every business by function,"* Wiley.

Fisk, Peter., (2010), *"People, Planet and Profit: how to embrace sustainability for innovation and business growth,"* Kogan Page.

Gates, Bill., (2022), *"How to Avoid a Climate Disaster: the solutions we have and the breakthroughs we need,"* Penguin.

Responsible Business.

Gentile, Mary. C., (2012), *"Giving Vices to Values: How to speak your mind when you know what's right,"* Yale University Press

Greenleaf, Robert. K., (2002), *"Servant Leadership: A journey into the nature of legitimate power and greatness,"* (25th edition), Paulist Press.

Hawken, Paul., (2018), *"Drawdown: the most comprehensive plan ever proposed to reverse global warming,"* Penguin.

Hawken, Paul., (2010), *"Ecology of Commerce: a declaration of sustainability,"* Harper Paperbacks.

Hollender, Jeffrey., & Breen, Bill., (2010), *"The Responsibility Revolution: How the next generation of businesses will win,"* John Wiley & Sons.

Hurst, Aaron., Hughes, Darryl, et.al. (2014), *"The Purpose Economy: How your desire for impact, personal growth and community is changing the world,"* Elevate.

Hutton, Will., (2015)., *"How Good Can We Be: Ending the mercenary society and building a great country,"* Little, Brown Book Group.

Kibirige, Alison. Dillion., & Kiryabwire, Tarinyeba., (2019), *"Corporate Governance Unlocked,"* CGI Publishing.

Klein, Naomi., (2015), *"This Changes Everything: capitalism vs the climate,"* Penguin.

Kopnina, Helen., & Blewitt, John., (2018), "Sustainable Business: key issues," Routledge.

Laloux, Frederic., (2014), *"Reinventing Organizations: a guide to creating organisations inspired by the next stage of human consciousness,"* Nelson Parker.

Responsible Business.

Levitt, Tom., (2015), *"Welcome to GoodCo: Using the tools of business to create public good,"* Routledge.

Lovins, L. Hunter., & Cohen, Boyd., (2012), *"The Way Out: kick-starting capitalism to save our economic arse,"* Hill and Wang.

Miller, Jon., & Parker, Lucy., (2013), *"Everybody's Business: The unlikely story of how big business can fix the world,"* Biteback Publishing.

Moyo, Dambisa., (2021), *"How Boards Work: and how they can work better in a chaotic world,"* The Bridge Street Press.

Peters, Tom., (2021), *"Excellence Now: Extreme Humanism,"* Networlding Publishing.

Pfeffer, Jeffrey., (2018), *"Dying for a Paycheck: How modern management harms employee health and company performance– and what we can do about it,"* Harper Business.

Raworth, Kate., (2018), *"Doughnut Economics: seven ways to think like a 21st Century economist,"* Random House Business.

Reitz, Megan., & Higgins, John., (2019), *"Speak Up: The how to guide to navigating the power and politics of conversations at work,"* FT Publishing International.

Richer, Julian., (2019), *"The Ethical Capitalist: How to make business work better for society,"* Random House Business.

Robertson, Brian. J., (2016), *"Holacracy: The Revolutionary Management System that abolishes Hierarchy."* Penguin Books

Responsible Business.

Sainsbury, David., (2013), *"Progressive Capitalism: How to achieve economic growth, liberty, and social justice,"* Biteback Publishing.

Shepherd, N. (2005) *"Governance, Accountability and Sustainable Development: An agenda for the 21st century,"* Thomson Carswell, Canada.

Shepherd, N. (2021) *"Corporate Culture – Combining Purpose and Values,"* Amazon KDP (Eduvision / Jannas Publications).

Shepherd, N. (2021), *"The Cost of Poor Culture: The massive financial opportunity in an enhanced workplace culture,"* Jannas Publications / Kindle Direct Publishing.

Shepherd. N., (2022), "Toxic Culture," Amazon KDP. Jannas Publications / Eduvision

Shepherd. N., & Smyth. Peter., (2012) *"Reflective Leaders and High-Performance Organizations,"* iUniverse Publishing.

Ton, Zeynep., (2014), *"The Good Jobs Strategy: How the smartest companies invest in employees to lower costs and boost profits,"* Amazon Publishing.

Tricker, Bob., (2019), *"Corporate Governance: principles, policies, and practices,"* Oxford University Press.

Wagner, Sigrun. M., (2020), *"Business and Environmental Sustainability: Foundations, challenges and corporate functions,"* Routledge.

Werbach, Adam., (2009)., *"Strategy for Sustainability: a business manifesto,"* Harvard Business Review Press.

Further work by the author

The author, Nick Shepherd has also written the following books, some of which are included in the bibliography. Several of them address corporate culture.

Non-fiction
Variance Analysis for Cost Performance Measurement (1980), Jannas Publications

Governance, Accountability and Sustainable Development: An agenda for the 21st Century (2005), Thomson Carswell

The Controllers Handbook (2nd. edition), 2008, CCH, a Wolters-Kluwer business

Reflective Leaders and High-Performance Organizations (jointly with Dr. Peter Smyth), 2012, iUniverse

How Accountants Lost Their Balance, 2021, Jannas Publications

Corporate Culture – Combining Purpose and Values, 2021, Jannas Publications

The Cost of Poor Culture, 2021, Jannas Publications

Toxic Culture, 2022, Jannas Publications

Understanding and Reporting Human Capital, 2021, Jannas Publications

Responsible Business.

Fiction
The Tunnels of Wallingford, 2021, Jannas Publications

No Fun at Great Toys, 2022, Jannas Publications

Fun Returns to Great Toys, 2022, Jannas Publications

Responsible Business.

Responsible Business.

Nick (A) Shepherd
Author

Experienced business professional, thinker, author, and futurist

Nick has over 50 years of varied work experience including senior general management and finance roles. From 1989 to 2018 he was active in his own management consulting and professional development company. Currently he still spends time on research and writing, that focuses in the areas of organizational sustainability, human capital, and integrated reporting. Nick has experience working in, and with private family business, public corporations, and governments and NPO's, both in Canada and internationally.

Since his (semi) retirement in late 2017 Nick has added to his books especially related to organizational culture and human aspects of business. Nick met Jim Bignal as a result of a discussion about one of his books on corporate culture, a meeting that turned into Nick's continuing involvement with, and commitment to the concept of Responsible Business.

Nick lives with his wife at an old 1923 log cabin, west of Ottawa, Ontario that sits close to the Ottawa river.

Contact Nick at nick@eduvision.ca

Responsible Business.

Jim Bignal
Advisor and Champion of Change
Founder Responsible Business,
Past Chair, Founder and CEO Cavendish Hospitality and Events

Jim spent most of his working career running the renowned corporate hospitality agency, Cavendish Hospitality and Events, from 1981 until his retirement in 2016. Cavendish won numerous official hospitality contracts including two Rugby World Cups, 1999 (Wales) and 2003 (Australia), the 2007 Cricket World Cup and the 2010 World T20 cricket both in the Caribbean. On Jim's retirement, Cavendish was bought by AOK Events in 2016.

In 2018, Jim co-founded Ethical Reading with Gurprit Singh with the objective of helping organisations in Reading do the right thing by each other, the wider community, and the environment. Ethical Reading is looking to maximise the positive change it is creating in Reading by helping to establish ethical hubs in different towns and cities throughout the UK and beyond, kick-starting an Ethical Cities Movement.

Responsible Business.

Since 2020, Jim has been working on the Responsible Business Project 2030 which has a mission to make responsible business commonplace by 2030 and taught in schools throughout the world.

Jim lives with his wife, Virginia, in the Reading area and they enjoy spending time with their four children and five grandchildren. Jim plays golf and after a promising debut at the age 14, his play has got progressively worse ever since.